THE
# CATHOLIC RELIGION

# THE
# CATHOLIC RELIGION

*Illustrated and Explained For*
CHILD, ADULT AND CONVERT

*Compiled by*

Msgr. J. H. Burbach

*"Oh how I have loved thy law, O Lord! It
is my meditation all the day. Through thy
commandment, thou hast made me wiser
than my enemies: for it is ever with me. I
have understood more than all my teachers:
because thy testimonies are my meditation.
I have had understanding above ancients:
because I have sought thy commandments."*
—Psalm 118:97-100

TAN BOOKS AND PUBLISHERS, INC.
Rockford, Illinois 61105

Nihil Obstat:    H. B. Ries
                 Censor Librorum
                 St. Francis, Wisconsin
                 November 24, 1928

Imprimatur:    ✠ Sebastian G. Messmer
               Archbishop of Milwaukee
               November 30, 1928

Imprimatur:    ✠ Samuel A. Stritch
               Archbishop of Milwaukee
               October 7, 1933

Scriptural quotations are from the Douay-Rheims version of the Bible.

Library of Congress Catalog Card No.: 92-60087

ISBN: 0-89555-457-7

Printed and bound in the United States of America.

TAN BOOKS AND PUBLISHERS, INC.
P.O. Box 424
Rockford, Illinois 61105
1993

"Take hold on instruction, leave it not: keep it, because it is thy life."

—*Proverbs* 4:13

# INTRODUCTION

There is no better recommendation for a textbook than the praise of teachers who have subjected it to the acid test of the classroom and the instruction class. The latent mistakes in the presentation of a subject in a textbook are brought to light under the demands of classroom experience. Father Burbach's THE CATHOLIC RELIGION has been subjected to this test and today enjoys the praise and commendations of those who have found it a help in the difficult work of catechetical instruction. That it has met a wide need is evident from the fact that teachers have found it a real help and children are attracted to follow its text easily from its well-chosen illustrations.

In analyzing this excellent text to discover the reasons for its wide appeal we find that the author, in presenting in simple language and with attractive illustrations the truths of Religion, has not departed from the catechetical traditions of the Church. By some who are ignorant of the history of Catholic catechetics it has been said that we have no methodology in the teaching of Religion. Attempts have been made to give us Courses in Religion which evidence a better knowledge of pedagogy than of Catholic Doctrine. Departing from the order and the manner of traditional catechetics, some modern authors have given us texts in which the emphasis is so placed that the resultant conceptions are perilously near the heretical. Others with fine good will have sinned against the principle which requires deep knowledge of the subject as an absolute condition for successful pedagogic methods. Father Burbach calls back to the centuries of experience of the Church and presents the truths of Religion in the traditional order. He does not forget, however, to marshall to his service new helps. The illustrations are a novelty in catechetical texts, which carry us back to the frescoes and the stained glass windows of the old churches of

Europe and the expressive symbolism developed by Christian art to help the catechist in days when the printing press was not known. These illustrations, in keeping with the finest catechetic traditions, are just the use in new materials of old and tried pedagogic helps in the hands of the catechist. This novelty is one of the charms of the text, and its helpfulness cannot be overestimated in an age when the mind is reached so widely through the eye. The nice use of appropriate texts from Sacred Scripture is an interesting feature of this book. We have been accustomed to read certain Scripture texts in catechetical texts as proofs of doctrines, but the author of this text has used them with fine discrimination to illustrate the truths that he presents and to initiate the student into the beauties of the Sacred Books. In simple, clear language the truths of the Church are presented in a way that avoids the use of unnecessary latinisms and theological terms without failing to give the special vocabulary necessary for a Catholic. There are neither too great concessions to the group that would deny the child his rightful Catholic vocabulary nor an unnecessary use of theological terms which fail to convey a meaning to the child.

We hope sincerely that this little book will enjoy wide use among those engaged in the work of instructing children and adults in Catholic Teaching. It deserves to be used by them for its excellences and close adherence to our best catechetical traditions. Particularly today, when texts in catechetics are being published by scholars who have neither the training for teaching religion nor the mandate to teach Religion, it is consoling to commend a book written by a priest who is conscious of his great mission of teaching the truths of Catholic Teaching and approaches his task with preparation and an appreciation of its difficulties.

✠ SAMUEL A. STRITCH
Archbishop of Milwaukee

October 7, 1933

# PREFACE

This book is a brief and simple exposition of our relations towards God as taught by the Catholic Church.

It comprises three principal parts.

The First Part teaches us the chief truths of religion as we find them in the Apostles' Creed.

The Second Part teaches us a rule of conduct as laid down in the Commandments of God and the Precepts of the Church.

The Third Part teaches us the means given to us by God to *receive, preserve,* and *increase* the divine life in our souls.

*"Now this is eternal life: That they may know Thee, the only true God, and Jesus Christ, Whom Thou hast sent." (John* 17:3).

# CONTENTS

## PART I

1

# PART II

# PART III

# PART I

*The first part of this book teaches us the chief truths of religion as we find them in the Apostles' Creed.*

## THE SIGN OF THE CROSS

In the name of the Father, and of the Son, and of the Holy Ghost. Amen.

## THE OUR FATHER

Our Father, Who art in Heaven, hallowed be Thy name: Thy kingdom come; Thy will be done on earth, as it is in Heaven. Give us this day our daily bread: and forgive us our trespasses, as we forgive those who trespass against us. And lead us not into temptation; but deliver us from evil. Amen.

## THE HAIL MARY

Hail Mary, full of grace, the Lord is with thee; blessed art thou among women, and blessed is the fruit of thy womb, Jesus. Holy Mary, Mother of God, pray for us sinners, now and at the hour of our death. Amen.

## THE GLORY BE TO THE FATHER

Glory be to the Father, and to the Son, and to the Holy Ghost. As it was in the beginning, is now, and ever shall be, world without end. Amen.

## AN ACT OF CONTRITION

O My God, I am heartily sorry for having offended Thee, and I detest all my sins, because I dread the loss of Heaven and the pains of Hell, but most of all because they offend Thee, my God, Who art all good and deserving of all my love. I firmly resolve, with the help of Thy grace, to confess my sins, to do penance, and to amend my life. Amen.

## THE APOSTLES' CREED

The chief truths or teachings of the Catholic religion are to be found in the Apostles' Creed.

The Apostles' Creed is commonly divided into twelve parts called articles.

## THE APOSTLES' CREED

Art. 1. I believe in God, the Father Almighty, Creator of Heaven and earth;

2. and in Jesus Christ, His only Son, our Lord;

3. Who was conceived by the Holy Ghost; born of the Virgin Mary;

4. suffered under Pontius Pilate, was crucified, died, and was buried;

5. He descended into Hell; the third day He arose again from the dead;

6. He ascended into Heaven; sitteth at the right hand of God, the Father Almighty;

7. from thence He shall come to judge the living and the dead;

8. I believe in the Holy Ghost;

9. the Holy Catholic Church, the Communion of Saints;

10. the forgiveness of sins;

11. the resurrection of the body;

12. and life everlasting. Amen.

## FAITH

Faith is a gift given to us by God by which we firmly believe all that He has revealed.

If we wish to reach Heaven, we must have Faith.

St. Paul says: *"Without Faith it is impossible to please God."* (*Heb.* 11:6).

Christ says: *"He that believeth not, shall be condemned."* (*Mark* 16:16).

The true Faith is to be found in the Catholic Church alone, because She teaches all that Christ taught.

*"He that heareth you, heareth Me."* (*Luke* 10:16).

Jesus Christ founded His Church, that His teachings might be preserved in Her for all generations.

*"Going therefore, teach ye all nations."* (*Matt.* 28:19).

Faith is a gift for which we must always pray, for God gives it to us out of His own pure Goodness.

*"Without Me you can do nothing."* (*John* 15:5).

The chief things which we must believe are contained in the Apostles' Creed.

**CATHOLICS PROFESS THEIR FAITH BY
THE SIGN OF THE CROSS.**

*"In the name of the Father, and of the Son, and of the Holy
Ghost. Amen." (Matt. 28:19).*

*"But the Paraclete, the Holy Ghost, Whom the Father will send in My name, He will teach you all things, and bring all things to your mind, whatsoever I shall have said to you." (John 14:26).*

## THE FOUR EVANGELISTS

ST. MATTHEW     ST. MARK     ST. LUKE     ST. JOHN

## THE BIBLE

The Bible is a collection of Books written by Moses, the Prophets, the Evangelists, and others under the inspiration of the Holy Ghost, and received by the Church as the inspired and revealed word of God.

The Bible is divided into two parts: the Old and New Testament.

The Old Testament contains the inspired Books written before the coming of Jesus Christ.

The New Testament contains the inspired Books written after the coming of Jesus Christ.

We must believe all that is contained in the Bible, because it is the word of God, Who is the infallible truth.

1. Christ teaching. (*Matt.* 5, 6, 7).
2. St. Peter teaching. (*Acts* 15:7-11).
3. St. Paul teaching. (*Acts* 17:22-31).
4. St. Patrick preaching in the fifth century what Christ and the Apostles had taught.

## TRADITION

Tradition is the unwritten word of God, handed down to us by word of mouth from Jesus Christ and the Apostles.

St. Paul writes regarding Tradition: *"Therefore, brethren, stand fast; and hold the Traditions which you have learned, whether by word, or by our epistle."* (*2 Thess.* 2:14).

The Catholic Church has preserved Tradition unaltered, as the records of history prove.

In Tradition we must recognize the same authority that we recognize in the Bible, God the Eternal Truth.

*"He that heareth you, heareth Me; and he that despiseth you, despiseth Me; and he that despiseth Me, despiseth Him that sent Me."* (*Luke* 10:16).

## THE FIRST ARTICLE OF THE CREED

*I believe in God, the Father Almighty,*
*Creator of Heaven and earth.*

### GOD

God is a Spirit, infinitely perfect.
*"God is a Spirit; and they that adore Him, must adore*
*Him in Spirit and in Truth." (John 4:24).*

We call God a *Spirit*, because He has understanding
and free will, but no body.

God is an infinitely perfect Spirit, because He includes
in Himself all perfections without limit.

The principal perfections of God are: He is eternal,
everywhere, all-knowing, all-wise, almighty; infinitely holy,
just, good, merciful, true, faithful, and provident.

God is *eternal* means that He is without beginning and
without end.

God is *everywhere* means that He is in Heaven, on
earth, and in all places.

God is *all-knowing* means that He knows all things,
past, present, and future, and even our most secret
thoughts and desires.

God is *all-wise* means that He knows how to do things
in the best way.

God is *almighty* means that He can do all things.

God is *holy* means that He loves and wills only what is good, and hates what is evil.

God is *just* means that He rewards every good deed and punishes every evil deed.

God is *good* means that He gives us numberless graces and blessings.

God is *merciful* means that He pardons us if we are sincerely sorry for our sins.

God is *true* means that He can neither deceive nor be deceived.

God is *faithful* means that He keeps His promises and carries out His threats.

God is *provident* means that He watches over us, and cares for all His creatures with fatherly goodness and wisdom.

## THE TRINITY

We believe that there is but one God.
*"I am the Lord thy God. Thou shalt not have strange gods before Me." (Ex.* 20:2,3).

Our reason tells us that there can be but one God.
If there were two Gods, neither of them could be infinite; therefore, neither of them could be God.

We believe that there are three Persons in one God: the Father, the Son, and the Holy Ghost.

We believe that each of these three Persons is God; that is, that the Father is God, the Son is God, and the Holy Ghost is God.

We know that there are three Persons in God from our Lord Jesus Christ, Who told His Apostles to baptize all nations: *"In the name of the Father, and of the Son, and of the Holy Ghost." (Matt.* 28:19).

How it is possible that there are three Persons in God is a mystery.
Even nature is full of mysteries: the little apple-seed produces a tree, a blossom, and an apple.
Who can understand this mystery?

We believe that the three divine Persons are equally powerful and perfect.
*"And there are three who give testimony in Heaven, the Father, the Word, and the Holy Ghost. And these three are one." (1 Jn.* 5:7).
By analogy we attribute to the Father our creation, to the Son our redemption, and to the Holy Ghost our sanctification.

## THE BLESSED TRINITY

*"There are three who give testimony in Heaven, the Father, the Word, and the Holy Ghost. And these three are one." (1 Jn. 5:7).*

## CREATION

The Bible tells us that God created Heaven and earth, and all things.

*"In the beginning God created heaven and earth."* (*Gen.* 1:1).

To *create* means to make something out of nothing.

God created all things for His own honor and glory, and for the good of His creatures.

*"The Lord hath made all things for Himself."* (*Prov.* 16:4).

*"Holy, holy, holy the Lord God of Hosts, all the earth is full of His glory."* (*Is.* 6:3).

God not only created the world, He also preserves it and watches over it with fatherly goodness and wisdom.

*"Casting all your care upon Him, for He hath care of you."* (*1 Ptr.* 5:7).

The care which God takes of the world is called *Divine Providence.*

God permits sin in the world, because He has given man a free will.

God permits evil in the world that He might draw good from it.

Sufferings and troubles are good for the sinner and the just.

They are a means of conversion for the sinner.

They are opportunities to gain greater merit for the just.

*"Whom the Lord loveth, He chastiseth."* (*Heb.* 12:6).

That God often draws good out of evil can be seen from the history of Joseph of Egypt, and the crucifixion of the Son of God. (*Gen.* 37; *1 Jn.* 2:2).

**THE CREATION**
*Gen.* 1:1, 26.

## THE ANGELS

The angels are pure spirits, that is, without a body, created to adore God and enjoy Heaven.

God created the angels good and happy, but not all of them remained good and happy.

A large number of the angels rebelled against God, and God cast them into Hell forever.

These angels wanted to be just as great as God.

They are called the bad angels or devils.

God rewarded the good angels for their fidelity, and gave them happiness in Heaven forever.

Not only did God create the angels to adore Him and assist before His throne, He also used them at different times as His messengers to men, and appointed a Guardian Angel for every person.

*"For He hath given His angels charge over thee; to keep thee in all thy ways."* (*Ps.* 90:11).

We should, therefore, pray to our Guardian Angel every day, especially in the morning and before we retire at night.

We must always be on our guard against the bad angels or devils.

They seek to harm us and lead us into sin.

The bad angels hate God, and are jealous of the eternal happiness He has promised to those who remain good.

## THE ANGELS

*"For He hath given His Angels charge over thee."*
(*Ps.* 90:11).

## THE CREATION AND FALL OF MAN

The first man and woman were Adam and Eve. They are commonly called our first parents.

The Bible tells us that God created the body of Adam out of the earth, and breathed an immortal soul into it. (*Gen.* 2:7).
He formed the body of Eve from a rib of Adam while he slept. (*Gen.* 2:22).

The soul is an immortal spirit, created by God after His own image and likeness.
*"Let us make man to our image and likeness."* (*Gen.* 1:26).

The soul's likeness to God consists in this, that it is immortal, and endowed with understanding and free will.

In the beginning Adam and Eve were good and happy, for God created them just and holy, and placed them in an earthly Paradise. (*Gen.* 2:15).

*The special gifts which God gave to Adam and Eve were:*
Sanctifying Grace;
A constant state of innocence in this life; and
The right to eternal glory in Heaven.

But Adam and Eve did not always remain good and happy.
They disobeyed God by eating of the forbidden fruit.
*"But of the tree of the Knowledge of good and evil, thou shalt not eat. For in what day soever thou shalt eat of it, thou shalt die the death."* (*Gen.* 2:17).

THE TEMPTATION AND FALL OF ADAM AND EVE
(*Gen. 3.*)

*On account of their sin of disobedience, God punished Adam and Eve:*

By depriving them of the gifts of Sanctifying Grace, innocence, and eternal happiness;

By driving them out of the Garden of Paradise;

By darkening their mind and weakening their will with regard to good and evil; and

By dooming them to suffering, work, and death.

Adam and Eve not only lost these gifts for themselves, but also for the whole human race.

This sin with all its evil consequences is inherited by everyone that comes into the world.

It is called Original Sin.

We can understand why all the children of Adam and Eve should inherit this sin.

If a very wealthy man gave a million dollars to a poor father, the father and his children would become very rich. But if the father were to lose this money in some way, not only he, but also his children would return to poverty.

The only person whom God has preserved from Original Sin is the Blessed Virgin Mary.

She was preserved from Original Sin, because she was chosen to be the Mother of the Redeemer.

The Virgin Mary's preservation from this sin is called her Immaculate Conception.

This Feast is celebrated on December 8.

God, however, did not abandon man in his fall; from the beginning He promised him a Redeemer. (*Gen.* 3:15).

THE BLESSED VIRGIN MARY WAS CONCEIVED
WITHOUT ORIGINAL SIN. (*Gen.* 3:15).

## THE SECOND ARTICLE OF THE CREED

*And in Jesus Christ His only Son, our Lord.*

The Redeemer, Whom God promised to Adam and Eve, came about four thousand years after their fall.

The promised Redeemer, as we know from the Bible and Tradition, is the only Son of God, Jesus Christ our Lord. (*John* 4:25-26).

The word Jesus means *Redeemer or Saviour.*
*"Thou shalt call His name Jesus; for He shall save His people from their sins."* (*Matt.* 1:21).

The word Christ means *Anointed.*
In the Old Testament the high-priests, kings, and prophets were anointed with oil.
Jesus Christ is the great High-priest, the King of kings, and the Prophet of prophets.

We know and believe that Jesus Christ is the promised Redeemer, because in Him were fulfilled all that the Prophets foretold about the coming Redeemer.

The Prophet Micheas foretold that the Redeemer would be born in Bethlehem. (*Mich.* 5:2).
The Prophet Isaias foretold that He was to be a great worker of miracles, and a teacher of the people. (*Is.* 35:5-7, *Is.* 49:1-6).
The Prophet Zacharias foretold that His disciples were to forsake Him at the time of His Passion. (*Zach.* 13:7).
The Prophet Ezechiel foretold the foundation and duration of His Church. (*Ezech.* 37:26).

### THE TRANSFIGURATION OF JESUS CHRIST
### ON MOUNT TABOR

*"And as he was yet speaking, behold a bright cloud over-shadowed them. And lo, a voice out of the cloud, saying: This is My beloved Son, in Whom I am well pleased: hear ye Him."* (Matt. 17:5).

We call Jesus Christ the *only Son of God,* because He is by nature and from all eternity the *only Son* of God, the Father.

*We know that Jesus Christ is the Son of God:*
From the testimony of His Heavenly Father;
From His own testimony;
From the testimony of His Apostles; and
From the constant teaching of the Catholic Church.

*The testimony of the Heavenly Father:*
At the Baptism and Transfiguration of Christ, the voice of the Father declared in the heavens: *"This is My beloved Son, in Whom I am well pleased."* (*Matt.* 3:17; 17:5).

*The testimony of Jesus Christ:*
To the words of the High-priest Caiphas, *"I adjure Thee by the Living God, that Thou tell us if Thou be Christ the Son of God,"* Jesus answered: *"Thou hast said it."* (*Matt.* 26:63, 64).

*The testimony of the Apostles:*
To the words of Christ, *"But whom do you say that I am?"* Peter answered: *"Thou art Christ, the Son of the living God."* (*Matt.* 16:16).

*The testimony of the Catholic Church:*
The Catholic Church has always firmly taught that Jesus Christ is the Son of God.

History proves that She has ever defended this doctrine as the chief doctrine of Christianity.

## JESUS CHRIST IS THE SON OF GOD

1. *"This is My beloved Son, in Whom I am well pleased." (Matt. 3:17).*

2. *"I adjure Thee by the living God, that Thou tell us if Thou be Christ the Son of God? Jesus saith to him: Thou hast said it."* (*Matt.* 26:63, 64).

3. *"Thomas answered, and said to Him: My Lord, and my God." (John* 20:28).

4. St. Paul proclaiming his belief in Jesus Christ, the Son of God, before King Agrippa. (*Acts* 26).

## THE THIRD ARTICLE OF THE CREED

*Who was conceived by the Holy Ghost,
born of the Virgin Mary.*

### THE INCARNATION OF JESUS CHRIST

By the *Incarnation* of Jesus Christ we mean that He was made man.

Jesus Christ was made man by the overshadowing power of the Holy Ghost, and was born of the Virgin Mary. (*Luke* 1:35).

Jesus Christ is both *true God* and *true man.*
He is *true God* means that He is the true and only Son of God, the Father.
He is *true man* means that He is the Son of the Blessed Virgin Mary, and has a soul and body like ours.

There are therefore two natures in Jesus Christ: the *nature of God* because He is God, and the *nature of man* because He became man.

We believe that there is but one Person in Jesus Christ, the Second Divine Person of the Blessed Trinity.
Jesus Christ is God from eternity, He became man in time.

The Blessed Virgin Mary is truly the Mother of God, because the same Divine Person who is the Son of God is her Son.

The Bible tells us that St. Joseph was the spouse of the Virgin Mary, and the foster-father of the Child Jesus. (*Luke* 2:49).

The Son of God became man in order to suffer and die for us. (*Matt.* 1:21).
As God He could neither suffer nor die.

## THE ANNUNCIATION

*"And the angel being come in, said unto her: Hail, full of grace, the Lord is with thee: blessed art thou among women."* (*Luke* 1:28).

## THE BIRTH AND CHILDHOOD OF JESUS CHRIST

Jesus Christ was born in a stable at Bethlehem some two thousand years ago.

An angel of the Lord announced the birth of the Child Jesus to shepherds, who were watching their sheep.

Hearing the glad news, the shepherds said to one another: *"Let us go over to Bethlehem, and let us see this word that is come to pass."* (*Luke* 2:15).

Not long after the Child Jesus was born, wise men came from the East, asking: *"Where is He that is born King of the Jews? For we have seen His star in the east, and are come to adore Him."* (*Matt.* 2:2).

The wise men found the Child at Bethlehem: *"Falling down, they adored Him; and opening their treasures, they offered Him gifts; gold, frankincense, and myrrh."* (*Matt.* 2:11).

When the new-born Redeemer was eight days old, He was circumcised, and was called *"Jesus."* (*Luke* 2:21).

When the Child Jesus was forty days old, His Mother Mary offered Him to God in the Temple, as was commanded by the laws of the Jews. (*Luke* 2:22).

When Herod, the King of Judea, heard that the promised Redeemer was born at Bethlehem, and that the wise men from the East called Him *"King of the Jews,"* he became very jealous.

In his jealousy he ordered all the boys of Bethlehem, within the age of two years, to be murdered. (*Matt.* 2:2-16).

But at this very same time, an angel of the Lord appeared to St. Joseph in sleep, and told him to take the Child and His Mother and hasten into Egypt. (*Matt.* 2:13).

**THE BIRTH OF JESUS CHRIST** *(Luke 2)*

The world celebrates this event on Christmas Day, Dec. 25.

After Herod's death Mary and Joseph returned from their exile in Egypt, and made their home at Nazareth. (*Matt.* 2:19-23).

When Jesus was twelve years old, He went with Mary and Joseph to Jerusalem to keep the Jewish Feast of the Passover.

On the way home He was lost for three days.

On the third day Mary and Joseph found Him in the Temple at Jerusalem in the midst of the teachers of the Jews.

These men were astonished at His wisdom, His questions, and His answers.

When Mary asked Jesus: *"Son, why hast Thou done so to us?"* He answered: *"Did you not know that I must be about My Father's business?"* (*Luke* 2:48, 49).

He meant His Heavenly Father's business.

Jesus then returned to Nazareth with Mary and Joseph and was subject to them.

After this event we hear nothing more of Him until He begins His public life at the age of thirty.

## THE CHILDHOOD, YOUTH, AND PUBLIC LIFE
## OF JESUS CHRIST

1. The shepherds at Bethlehem. (*Luke* 2:8-18).

2. The Wise Men from the East. (*Matt.* 2:1-12).

3. The flight into Egypt. (*Matt.* 2:13).

4. The Child Jesus in the Temple at the age of twelve. (*Luke* 2:41-51).

5. St. John the Baptist preparing the way of the Lord. (*Luke* 3).

6. The Baptism of Jesus Christ by St. John the Baptist. (*Luke* 3:21).

## THE PUBLIC LIFE OF JESUS CHRIST

When Jesus was thirty years old, He went to John the Baptist at the river Jordan to be baptized. (*Matt.* 3:13).
John the Baptist was preparing the way of the Lord.
Jesus allowed Himself to be baptized to give us a good example.

After His baptism Jesus went into the desert for forty days and forty nights.
He went there to pray and fast, and to prepare Himself for His public life.
In the desert He was tempted by the devil. (*Matt.* 4).

From the beginning of His public life, Jesus began to teach and gather disciples about Himself.
From His disciples He chose twelve Apostles. (*Mark* 3:13-19).
The word Apostle means *messenger.*

The twelve Apostles whom Jesus chose were: Peter, Andrew, James, John, Philip, Bartholomew, Matthew, Thomas, James the Less, Simon the Zealot, Jude, and Judas Iscariot. (*Luke* 6:13-16).

Jesus went about teaching for three years.
He often spoke to large gatherings of people, as in the case of the miraculous multiplication of the loaves. (*John* 6).
He often spoke in parables. (*Matt.* 13:34).

Jesus taught everything that we must believe, hope for, and do in order to be saved.
*"I am the Way, and the Truth, and the Life."* (*John* 14:6).

## CHRIST, THE TEACHER

1. Jesus teaching the children. (*Matt.* 18).

2. Jesus teaching in the temple. (*John* 7).

3. Jesus teaching the Samaritan or gentile woman. (*John* 4:1-28).

4. Jesus teaching the Scribes and Pharisees. (*Matt.* 22:15-22).

5. Jesus preaching the Sermon on the Mount. (*Matt.* 5, 6, 7).

6. Jesus acclaimed as Teacher and Prophet on the first Palm Sunday. (*Mark* 11:1-10).

*Jesus proved His mission as Teacher:*
By the holiness of His life;
By His miracles; and
By His prophecies.

*The holiness of Jesus' life:*
The traitor Judas confessed that he had shed "innocent
blood." (*Matt.* 27:4).
Pontius Pilate could find no cause in Christ. (*John*
18:38).
Christ Himself challenged the Jews: *"Which of you
shall convince [that is, convict] Me of sin?"* (*John*
8:46).

*The chief miracles of Jesus:*
He changed water into wine (*John* 2:1-11);
He stilled the storm and wind (*Matt.* 8:23-27);
He fed over five thousand people with five loaves and
two fish (*John* 6:1-14);
He healed the sick (*Mark* 2:1-12); and
He raised the dead to life. (*John* 11).

*The chief prophecies of Jesus:*
He foretold the betrayal of Judas (*Matt.* 26:21);
The denial of Peter (*Luke* 22:34);
His Resurrection from the dead (*Matt.* 26:61);
His Ascension into Heaven (*John* 20:17); and
The Descent of the Holy Ghost. (*John* 14:26).

That the Jewish people acclaimed Jesus as a great
Teacher can be seen from His triumphant entry into
Jerusalem shortly before His Passion and death. (*Mark*
11:1-10).
We celebrate this event on Palm Sunday.

## CHRIST, THE MIRACLE-WORKER

1. Jesus changes water into wine at Cana. (*John* 2:1-11).

2. Jesus feeds five thousand people with five loaves of bread and two fishes. (*John* 6:1-14).

3. Jesus heals the man sick of the palsy. (*Mark* 2:1-12).

4. Jesus saves Peter from drowning. (*Matt.* 14:25 31).

5. Jesus brings the daughter of Jairus back to life. (*Matt.* 9:18-26).

6. Jesus raises Lazarus to life. (*John* 11).

## THE FOURTH ARTICLE OF THE CREED

*Suffered under Pontius Pilate, was crucified,
died and was buried.*

*The principal sufferings of Jesus were:*
The agony in the Garden of Olives;
The mockery by the Jews and the soldiers;
The scourging at the pillar;
The crowning with thorns;
The Way of the Cross; and
The Crucifixion.

After the Last Supper, Jesus was taken prisoner by
the Jews under the leadership of Judas, who sold Him to
the Pharisees for thirty pieces of silver. (*Matt.* 26:14-15).

Jesus was condemned to death by the Roman governor,
Pontius Pilate. (*John* 19:16).

He was crucified on Mount Calvary near Jerusalem on
Good Friday, and died at three o'clock in the afternoon.
(*Luke* 23:33, 44, 46).

While Jesus was dying on the Cross, the sun was dark-
ened; the earth trembled; rocks were rent; graves were
opened; and the dead appeared to many. (*Matt.* 27:51-53).

*Jesus was not compelled to suffer and die.*
He suffered and died by His own free will.

He suffered and died to offer satisfaction for Original
Sin and the sins of all mankind, and to regain eternal happiness for men. (*Matt.* 1:21).

When Jesus was dead, His body was taken down from
the Cross and placed into a tomb. (*Matt.* 27:59-60).

## THE PASSION AND DEATH OF JESUS CHRIST

1. Jesus changes bread and wine into His Body and Blood at the Last Supper. (*Luke* 22:19, 20).

2. The agony of Jesus in the Garden of Olives. (*Mark* 14:32-42).

3. Jesus is betrayed by Judas with a kiss. (*Mark* 14:43-50).

4. Jesus before Pontius Pilate. (*Mark* 15).

5. The Way of the Cross. (*Mark* 15:20-23).

6. Jesus is crucified on Mount Calvary. (*Mark* 15:24-47).

## THE FIFTH ARTICLE OF THE CREED

*He descended into hell; the third day*
*He arose again from the dead.*

### THE DESCENT INTO LIMBO

After Jesus Christ died on the Cross, His soul descended into Limbo.

The souls of the just who had died were in Limbo.

The souls of the just were in Limbo because Heaven had been closed through Original Sin.

*Jesus Christ descended into Limbo:*
To comfort the souls of the just; and
To announce to them the joyful tidings of the Redemption.

While Jesus was dying on the Cross one of the thieves turned to Him and said: *"Lord, remember me when Thou shalt come into Thy kingdom."*
And Jesus replied to him: *"Amen I say to thee, this day thou shalt be with Me in Paradise."* (*Luke* 23:42-43).
When the soul of Jesus Christ entered Limbo, Limbo was changed into a Paradise.

The soul of Christ remained in Limbo until the third day.

### JESUS CHRIST DESCENDS INTO LIMBO

*"In which also coming He preached to those spirits that were in prison."* (*1 Ptr.* 3:19).

### ⸳ THE RESURRECTION OF JESUS CHRIST

Jesus Christ arose from the tomb in glory on the third day after His death.

He arose by His own Almighty Power.

The tomb had been sealed with a heavy stone and was guarded by Roman soldiers. (*Mark* 16:2-6).

Jesus Christ had foretold that He would arise from the dead.

*"Destroy this temple and in three days I will raise it up." (John* 2:19).

Jesus Christ arose from the tomb to prove that He is the Son of God, ánd that we are to rise again. (*1 Cor.* 15:13, 14).

Jesus Christ remained on earth forty days after His Resurrection.

He did this to prove that He was truly risen, and to instruct His Apostles. (*Acts* 1:2, 3).

During these forty days Jesus Christ often appeared to His Apostles and disciples.

He came to them through closed doors. (*John* 20:19).

He ate with them. (*John* 21:12).

He permitted them to touch His wounds. (*John* 20:27).

He conversed with them. (*John* 21:15).

At these different appearances Jesus Christ gave His Apostles the powers to teach, baptize, and forgive sins, and appointed Peter the visible Head of the Church.

We celebrate the Resurrection of Our Lord on Easter Sunday.

## THE RESURRECTION OF JESUS CHRIST
## FROM THE TOMB

*"And behold there was a great earthquake. For an angel of the Lord descended from heaven, and coming, rolled back the stone, and sat upon it.*

*"And his countenance was as lightning, and his raiment as snow.*

*"And for fear of him, the guards were struck with terror, and became as dead men." (Matt. 28:2-4).*

## THE SIXTH ARTICLE OF THE CREED

*He ascended into Heaven; sitteth at
the right hand of God, the Father Almighty.*

On the fortieth day after His Resurrection, Jesus
Christ ascended into Heaven.

*"And the Lord Jesus, after He had spoken to them, was
taken up into Heaven, and sitteth on the right hand of
God." (Mark 16:19).*

Jesus Christ ascended into Heaven from the Mount of
Olives, in the sight of His beloved Mother, Apostles, disciples, and friends. (*Acts* 1:10-14).

Jesus Christ ascended into Heaven by His own divine
power.

He ascended into Heaven with body and soul, taking
with Him the souls who were detained in Limbo.

*Jesus Christ ascended into Heaven:*
To enter into His Kingdom (*John* 18:36);
To send down the Holy Ghost (*John* 14:16);
To be our Mediator with His Father (*John* 14:14); and
To prepare an eternal dwelling for us. (*John* 14:2).

Jesus Christ *sitteth at the right hand of God, the Father
Almighty* means that as man He has power over all
creatures.

It means that as man He is next in honor to God.

*"All power is given to Me in Heaven and in earth."*
(*Matt.* 28:18).

We celebrate the feast of the Ascension of Our Lord
into Heaven on Ascension Thursday, forty days after
Easter.

## JESUS CHRIST ASCENDS INTO HEAVEN

*"And it came to pass, whilst He blessed them, He departed from them, and was carried up to Heaven.*

*"And they adoring went back into Jerusalem with great joy."* (*Luke* 24:51, 52).

## THE SEVENTH ARTICLE OF THE CREED

*From thence He shall come to judge the living and the dead.*

### THE PARTICULAR JUDGMENT

There are two kinds of Judgment, the Particular Judgment and the Last Judgment.

The Particular Judgment takes place immediately after a person dies.

The Last Judgment shall take place at the end of the world.

By the *Particular Judgment* we mean that God judges every person immediately after death.
*"It is appointed unto men once to die, and after this the Judgment."* (*Heb.* 9:27).

After the Particular Judgment the soul goes either to Heaven, Purgatory, or Hell.

The souls of those who die in the state of Sanctifying Grace, and are free from the temporal punishment due to sin, go after Particular Judgment to Heaven.

The souls of those who die in venial sin, or who are not free from the temporal punishment due to sin, go after Particular Judgment to Purgatory.

The souls of those who die in mortal sin go to Hell.

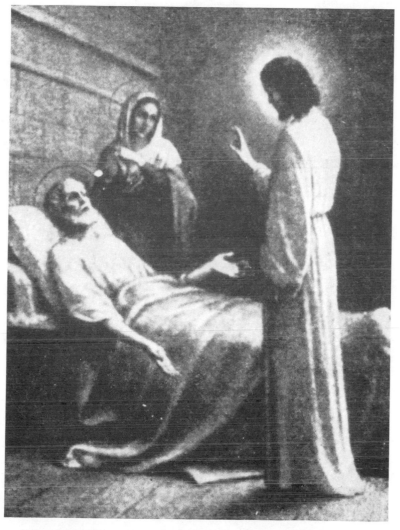

**"IT IS APPOINTED UNTO MEN ONCE TO DIE, AND AFTER THIS THE JUDGMENT." (*Heb.* 9:27).**

St. Joseph died in the presence of the Great Judge.

### THE LAST JUDGMENT

Jesus Christ shall come again at the end of the world with great power and majesty.

*"And then shall they see the Son of Man coming in the clouds, with great power and glory."* (*Mark* 13:26).

The purpose of the second coming of Jesus Christ shall be to judge the world.

This Judgment is called the *Last Judgment* or the General Judgment.

At the Last Judgment Jesus Christ shall make known to the whole world the good and evil of every person.

He shall show to the whole world the graces and opportunities that God gave everyone to save his soul.

To the good, Jesus Christ shall say: *"Come, ye blessed of My Father, possess you the kingdom prepared for you from the foundation of the world."* (*Matt.* 25:34).

To the wicked, He shall declare: *"Depart from Me, you cursed, into everlasting fire which was prepared for the devil and his angels."* (*Matt.* 25:41).

After the Last Judgment there shall be only Heaven and Hell.

## THE LAST JUDGMENT

*"For the Son of Man shall come in the glory of His Father with His Angels: and then will He render to every man according to his works."* (Matt. 16:27).

## THE EIGHTH ARTICLE OF THE CREED

*I believe in the Holy Ghost*

The Holy Ghost is the Third Person of the Blessed Trinity.

He is true God with the Father and the Son.

*"Going therefore, teach ye all nations; baptizing them in the name of the Father, and of the Son, and of the Holy Ghost." (Matt.* 28:19).

The Holy Ghost proceeds from the Father and the Son. (*John* 15:26).

Jesus Christ promised to send the Holy Ghost to His Apostles and the Church.

*"But the Paraclete, the Holy Ghost, whom the Father will send in My name, He will teach you all things, and bring all things to your mind, whatsoever I shall have said to you." (John* 14:26).

The Holy Ghost came down upon the Apostles ten days after the Ascension of Jesus Christ.

He descended upon them in the form of tongues of fire. (*Acts* 2:3).

Jesus Christ sent the Holy Ghost to strengthen, teach, sanctify, and guide the Church. (*John* 14:16, 26).

The seven gifts of the Holy Ghost are: Wisdom, Understanding, Counsel, Fortitude, Knowledge, Piety, and Fear of the Lord. (*Is.* 11:2).

We celebrate the Descent of the Holy Ghost on Pentecost or Whit-Sunday.

## THE DESCENT OF THE HOLY GHOST

"And suddenly there came a sound from heaven, us of a mighty wind coming, and it filled the whole house where they were sitting.

"And there appeared to them parted tongues as it were of fire, and it sat upon every one of them.

"And they were all filled with the Holy Ghost." (Acts 2:2-4).

## THE NINTH ARTICLE OF THE CREED

*I believe in the Holy Catholic Church,
the Communion of Saints.*

## THE CHURCH

The Church is the congregation of all those who profess the faith of Jesus Christ, partake of the same Sacraments, and are governed by one visible Head, the Pope of Rome.

The word pope comes from the Latin word "papa," and means *father.*

Jesus Christ founded the Church.

To Peter He said: *"Thou art Peter and upon this rock I will build My Church."* (*Matt.* 16:18).

Jesus Christ is the Head of the Church, but He is Her invisible Head.

Since the Church is a visible organization, it was necessary for Christ to give Her also a visible Head.

Jesus Christ made St. Peter the first visible Head of the Church when He addressed these words to him: *"Thou art Peter, and upon this rock I will build My Church, and the gates of Hell shall not prevail against it."* (*Matt.* 16:18).

*"I will give to thee the keys of the Kingdom of Heaven. And whatsoever thou shalt bind on earth, it shall be bound also in Heaven; and whatsoever thou shalt loose on earth, it shall be loosed also in Heaven."* (*Matt.* 16:19).

*"Feed My lambs...feed My sheep."* (*John* 21:16, 17).

The visible Head of the Church today is the Pope of Rome, who is a direct successor in the Apostolic Office of St. Peter.

The records of History prove this.

The successors of the other Apostles are the Bishops of the Catholic Church.

The priests of the Church are the assistants of the Bishop.

Jesus Christ founded the Church to teach, govern, sanctify, and save all men.

*"He that heareth you, heareth Me; he that despiseth you, despiseth Me." (Luke 10:16).*

## PETER BECOMES THE FIRST VISIBLE HEAD OF THE CHURCH

1. *"From henceforth thou shalt catch men." (Luke 5:10).*

2. *"I will give to thee the keys of the Kingdom of Heaven." (Matt. 16:19).*

3. *"Feed My lambs...Feed My sheep." (John 21:16, 17).*

4. Peter presides over the Council of Jerusalem as the first visible Head of the Church. (Acts 15:7).

## THE FOUR MARKS OF THE CHURCH

The Church has four Marks by which She may be known as the true Church founded by Jesus Christ.

The four Marks of the Church are: She is One, Holy, Catholic, Apostolic.

*The Church is* ONE means that Her members
Believe the same doctrines;
Have the same Sacrifice; and
Are united under the same visible Head.

*The Church is* HOLY means that:
Her Founder, Her Doctrines, Her Commandments, and
Her Sacraments are holy; and that She leads Her
members to holiness.

*The Church is* CATHOLIC means:
That She was founded for all people;
That She teaches all nations; and
That She is spread over the whole world.
*"Going therefore, teach ye all nations."* (*Matt.* 28:19).

*The Church is* APOSTOLIC means:
That She teaches the doctrines and traditions of the
Apostles; and
That She is governed by their lawful successors.
*"Therefore, brethren, stand fast; and hold the Tradi-
tions which you have learned, whether by word, or
by our epistle."* (*2 Thess.* 2:14).

These four Marks are to be found in the Holy Roman Catholic Church alone.

## THE CHURCH IS ONE, HOLY, CATHOLIC, APOSTOLIC

1. St. Patrick in the fifth century preached the same doctrines taught by Christ and the Apostles, and still taught and believed by the Catholic Church today.

2. St. Francis of Assisi is one of the great Saints of the Catholic Church.

3. The Catholic Church is found in all parts of the world. Father Marquette crossed the Atlantic to help bring the glad tidings of the Faith of Christ to the American Indian.

4. The Catholic Church dates from the time of the Apostles. She has always taught the doctrines of the Apostles. And the records of History prove that Her bishops and priests are true successors of the Apostles.

## THE QUALITIES OF THE CHURCH

*The Catholic Church possesses three great qualities:*
She teaches with authority.
She is infallible in matters of Faith and Morals.
She is indefectible.

The Church *teaches with authority* means that the Pope and the Bishops, as successors of the Apostles, have the right to teach and govern the faithful.
*"All power is given to Me in Heaven and in Earth. Going therefore, teach ye all nations . . . teaching them to observe all things whatsoever I have commanded you."* (*Matt.* 28:18-20).

The Church *is infallible in matters of Faith and Morals* means that She cannot err when She teaches a doctrine of Faith and Morals.
*"But the Paraclete, the Holy Ghost, whom the Father will send in My name, He will teach you all things, and bring all things to your mind, whatsoever I shall have said to you."* (*John* 14:26).

The Church *is indefectible* means that Her enemies cannot destroy Her and that She will last to the end of time.
Christ declares: *"The gates of Hell shall not prevail against it."* (*Matt.* 16:18).
St. Paul calls the Church *"the pillar and ground of the Truth."* (*1 Tim.* 3:15).

1. ST. PETER'S CHURCH AT ROME, THE CENTER OF CATHOLICITY.

2. THE HIERARCHY OF THE CHURCH: POPE, BISHOP, PRIEST, DEACON.

## THE COMMUNION OF SAINTS

*To the Communion of Saints belong:*
The faithful on earth;
The souls in Purgatory; and
The Saints in Heaven.

The Communion of Saints means that its members help one another.

The faithful on earth help one another by prayer and good works.

The *faithful on earth* help the poor souls in Purgatory by prayer, good works, indulgences, and attendance at the Holy Sacrifice of the Mass.

The *souls in Purgatory* pray for the faithful on earth.

The *Saints in Heaven* intercede for the faithful on earth and the souls in Purgatory.

The faithful on earth are called the *Church Militant,* because they are still fighting the battles of life against the devil, the flesh, and the world.

The souls in Purgatory are called the *Church Suffering,* because they are still suffering for their sins in the purifying fires of Purgatory.

The Saints in Heaven are called the *Church Triumphant,* because they have successfully conquered all enemies, and are now enjoying the fruits of their victories.

The Church has appointed November 1 as All Saints' Day.

## THE COMMUNION OF SAINTS

### THE CHURCH IN HEAVEN
### THE CHURCH ON EARTH
### THE CHURCH IN PURGATORY

*"And if one member suffer any thing, all the members suffer with it; or if one member glory, all the members rejoice with it."* (*1 Cor.* 12:26).

## PURGATORY

Purgatory is the state in which those souls suffer for a time, who die in venial sin, or who have not satisfied for the temporal punishment due for sin.

*"There shall not enter into it [Heaven] any thing defiled."* (Apoc. 21:27).

Punishment is due for sin.

A mortal sin deserves an eternal punishment, and a venial sin a temporal punishment.

The Sacrament of Penance remits the guilt of sin and the eternal punishment due for mortal sin, but not all the temporal punishment due for mortal and venial sin.

The temporal punishment due to sin can be satisfied for in this life by good works; that is, by Attendance at the Holy Sacrifice of the Mass, Reception of the Sacraments, Indulgences, Almsgiving, Prayer, and Spiritual and Corporal Works of Mercy.

The Bible tells us that there is a Purgatory.

Judas Machabeus ordered sacrifices to be offered in Jerusalem for the sins of his fallen soldiers. (2 Mach. 12:43).

*"If any man's work burn, he shall suffer loss; but he himself shall be saved, yet so as by fire."* (1 Cor. 3:15).

The souls who are sent to Purgatory must remain there until the Justice of God has been satisfied.

The souls in Purgatory suffer willingly, because they are certain of their eternal salvation.

The Church has appointed November 2 as All Souls' Day.

## THE MASS FOR THE DEAD

*"It is therefore a holy and wholesome thought to pray for the dead, that they may be loosed from sins."* (2 Mach. 12:46).

The greatest prayer that can be offered up to God on behalf of the Souls in Purgatory is the Holy Sacrifice of the Mass.

## THE TENTH ARTICLE OF THE CREED

*(I believe in) the forgiveness of sins.*

God alone can forgive sins, and those to whom He has given this power.

In the tenth article of the Creed we confess our belief that Jesus Christ, the Son of God, conferred the power to forgive sins upon the Apostles and their successors, who are the Bishops and priests of the Catholic Church.

Jesus Christ instituted two Sacraments by which sins are forgiven, the Sacrament of Baptism and the Sacrament of Penance.

Jesus Christ conferred the power to baptize upon His Apostles with these words: *"Going therefore, teach ye all nations; baptizing them in the name of the Father, and of the Son, and of the Holy Ghost."* (*Matt.* 28:19).

Jesus Christ conferred the power to forgive sins in the Sacrament of Penance, when He said to His Apostles: *"Whose sins you shall forgive, they are forgiven them; and whose sins you shall retain, they are retained."* (*John* 20:23).

The Sacrament of Baptism forgives Original Sin, and the sins committed before Baptism.

The Sacrament of Penance forgives all sins committed after Baptism.

## JESUS CHRIST FORGIVES SIN

*"Wherefore I say to thee: Many sins are forgiven her, because she hath loved much.*

*"And He said to her: Thy sins are forgiven thee."* (*Luke* 7:47, 48).

## THE ELEVENTH ARTICLE OF THE CREED

*(I believe in) the resurrection of the body.*

By *the resurrection of the body* we mean that on the Last Day, Jesus Christ will raise the bodies of all men from the dead, and reunite them to the soul forever.

By *the resurrection of the body* we also mean that the just will arise to eternal glory and the wicked to everlasting damnation.

Jesus Christ foretold the resurrection of the body.
*"Wonder not at this, for the hour cometh, wherein all that are in the graves shall hear the voice of the Son of God. And they that have done good things, shall come forth unto the resurrection of life; and they that have done evil, unto the resurrection of judgment." (John 5:28, 29).*

The Resurrection of Jesus Christ from the tomb is a proof for the resurrection of the body.
*"But if there be no resurrection of the dead, then Christ is not risen again.*     ·
*"And if Christ be not risen again, then is our preaching vain, and your faith is also vain." (1 Cor. 15:13, 14).*

Jesus Christ also proved the doctrine of the resurrection of the body by bringing back to life: the daughter of Jairus, the son of the widow of Naim, and the brother of Mary and Martha.

## RESURRECTION FROM THE DEAD

1. *"He is not here, for He is risen, as He said."* (*Matt.* 28:6).

2. The risen Christ with two of His disciples at Emmaus. (*Luke* 24:13-35).

3. The doubting Thomas places his fingers into Christ's wounded side. (*John* 20:26-29).

4. Christ brings the daughter of Jairus back to life. (*Matt.* 9:23, 24, 25).

5. Christ raises to life the widow's son of Naim. (*Luke* 7:11-16).

6. Christ raises Lazarus to life. (*John* 11:1-45).

## THE TWELFTH ARTICLE OF THE CREED

*(I believe in) life everlasting.*

### HEAVEN

By *Life Everlasting* we mean that the just shall live forever in the glory and happiness of Heaven.
*"And these shall go into everlasting punishment; but the just, into life everlasting." (Matt.* 25:46).

The glory and happiness of Heaven consists in seeing, loving, and enjoying God forever.

St. Paul, who had a vision of Heaven, states: *"Eye hath not seen, nor ear heard, neither hath it entered into the heart of man, what things God hath prepared for them that love Him." (1 Cor.* 2:9).

The happiness of the blessed in Heaven is according to their merits.
*"For the Son of Man shall come in the glory of His Father with His Angels; and then will He render to every man according to his works." (Matt.* 16:27).

Only those can enter Heaven who are in the state of Sanctifying Grace, free from sin, and from the punishment due for sin.
*"There shall not enter into it any thing defiled." (Apoc.* 21:27).

Heaven is won by a life of self-denial.
*"Narrow is the gate, and strait is the way that leadeth to life." (Matt.* 7:14).

## HEAVEN

*"Let not your heart be troubled...*
*"In My Father's house there are many mansions." (John*
14:1, 2).

## HELL

We believe that the wicked shall live forever, and shall be punished for all eternity in the fire of Hell.

Jesus Christ taught that there is a Hell, and that the wicked shall be punished forever.

*"Then He shall say to them also that shall be on His left hand: depart from Me, you cursed, into everlasting fire which was prepared for the devil and his angels."* (*Matt.* 25:41).

Jesus Christ described Hell as a place where there is *"weeping and gnashing of teeth."* (*Matt.* 8:12).

He also calls it an *"unquenchable fire."* (*Mark* 9:44).

The torments of the damned are not alike.

They differ according to the number and gravity of their sins.

Those who die in mortal sin are condemned by God to Hell.

The thought of Hell should keep us from sin.

*"In all thy works remember thy last end, and thou shalt never sin."* (*Ecclus.* 7:40).

# PART II

*The second part of this book teaches us a rule of conduct as laid down in the Commandments of God and the Precepts of the Church.*

## THE COMMANDMENTS

It is not enough to belong to the Church and to believe in the teachings of Jesus Christ to be saved; we must also keep the Commandments of God and His Church.

*"If thou wilt enter into life, keep the Commandments."* (*Matt.* 19:17).

### THE TWO GREAT COMMANDMENTS OF LOVE

One day a Scribe asked Our Lord which is the first Commandment.

He answered: *"Thou shalt love the Lord thy God, with thy whole heart, and with thy whole soul...and with thy whole strength. This is the first commandment.*

*"And the second is like unto it: Thou shalt love thy neighbor as thyself. There is no other commandment greater than these."* (*Mark* 12:30, 31).

We should love God above all things because He is all-good, and because He created, redeemed, and sanctifies us, and daily gives us many graces.

*"Let us therefore love God, because God first hath loved us."* (*1 Jn.* 4:19).

We show that we love God by keeping the Commandments.

*"He that hath My commandments and keepeth them, he it is that loveth Me."* (*John* 14:21).

Our neighbor is everybody.

*We should love our neighbor:*
Because God loves him;
Because we are all created by the Heavenly Father;
Because God calls all men to be brothers and sisters
    of the Redeemer; and
Because Jesus Christ commands us to love him.
*"Love your enemies: do good to them that hate you: and pray for them that persecute and calumniate you."* (*Matt.* 5:44).

## THE CORPORAL WORKS OF MERCY

1. Jesus feeding the hungry by a miracle. (*Mark* 6:34-44).

2. Rebecca kindly offering a drink of water to the servant of Abraham. (*Gen.* 24:13-20).

3. The good Samaritan gladly clothed the man who fell among the robbers. (*Luke* 10:30-37).

4. The homeless prodigal son is given shelter by his forgiving father. (*Luke* 15:11-32).

5. Peter is visited by an Angel in prison, and miraculously delivered. (*Acts* 12:7-11).

6. Jesus heals one sick of the palsy. (*Matt.* 9:2).

7. Jesus was buried by Joseph of Arimathea and Nicodemus. (*John* 19:38-42).

*We show love to our enemies:*
By forgiving them from our hearts;
By helping them in their needs; and
By praying for them.
*"If you will not forgive men, neither will your Father forgive you your offenses." (Matt.* 6:15).

We must love ourselves, because God commands this.
*"Thou shalt love thy neighbor as thyself." (Mark* 12:31).

True love of one's self means to seek first and above all things our eternal happiness.
*"But seek ye first the kingdom of God and His justice." (Luke* 12:31).

The Bible gives us many beautiful examples of the love of neighbor and enemy.
These examples are explained in the Corporal and Spiritual Works of Mercy.

*The Corporal Works of Mercy:*
1. To feed the hungry;
2. To give drink to the thirsty;
3. To clothe the naked;
4. To give shelter to the homeless;
5. To visit the imprisoned;
6. To visit the sick;
7. To bury the dead.

*The Spiritual Works of Mercy:*
1. To warn sinners;
2. To instruct the ignorant;
3. To counsel the doubting;
4. To comfort the sorrowing;
5. To bear wrongs patiently;
6. To forgive wrongs;
7. To pray for the living and the dead.

## THE SPIRITUAL WORKS OF MERCY

1. St. John the Baptist warning the sinners. (*Luke* 3:1-18).

2. Jesus instructing the ignorant in His Sermon on the Mount. (*Matt.* 5).

3. The risen Lord counsels the doubting Mary Magdalene. (*John* 20:1-18).

4. The holy women who came to the tomb to anoint Jesus are comforted in their sorrow by an angel with the news that Jesus is risen. (*Mark* 16:1-7).

5. Jesus bears our wrongs with supreme patience. (*John* 19:4-6).

6. *"Father forgive them, for they know not what they do." (Luke* 23:34).

7. The Holy Sacrifice of the Mass is offered for the living and the dead.

## THE TEN COMMANDMENTS OF GOD

*The ten Commandments of God are:*

1. I am the Lord thy God. Thou shalt not have strange gods before Me.

2. Thou shalt not take the name of the Lord thy God in vain.

3. Remember that thou keep holy the Sabbath Day.

4. Honor thy father and thy mother.

5. Thou shalt not kill.

6. Thou shalt not commit adultery.

7. Thou shalt not steal.

8. Thou shalt not bear false witness against thy neighbor.

9. Thou shalt not covet thy neighbor's wife.

10. Thou shalt not covet thy neighbor's goods. (*Ex.* 20).

God gave the ten Commandments to Moses on Mount Sinai.

The ten Commandments are an explanation of the two great Commandments of the love of God and neighbor.

The ten Commandments were written on two tables of stone.

The three Commandments that comprise our duties towards God were written on the first stone.

The seven Commandments which comprise our duties towards our neighbor were written on the second stone.

Jesus Christ declares that we cannot enter Heaven unless we keep the Commandments.

*"But if thou wilt enter into life, keep the Commandments."* (*Matt.* 19:17).

MOSES RECEIVING THE TEN COMMANDMENTS
FROM GOD (*Ex.* 19, 20).

### THE FIRST COMMANDMENT OF GOD

The first Commandment is: *I am the Lord thy God. Thou shalt not have strange gods before Me.*

In the first Commandment God obliges us to pay Him due honor and adoration.

We owe God two kinds of honor, an inward honor or the honor of our soul; and an outward honor, or the honor of our body.

*We honor God inwardly:*
By believing in Him;
By hoping in Him;
By loving Him; and
By adoring Him.

*We honor God outwardly:*
By professing our Faith publicly, that is, by going to
church, kneeling in prayer, etc.

We *believe in God* when we hold as true all that He has revealed.

*We sin against faith in God:*
By doubting in matters of faith (skepticism);
By not believing everything (heresy, schism);
By not believing at all (infidelity);
By giving up the Faith (apostasy).

We *hope in God* when we trust firmly that He will give us all that He has promised.

**THE ISRAELITES FALL INTO IDOLATRY AND
WORSHIP A GOLDEN CALF. (*Ex.* 32).**

*We sin against hope in God:*
By not hoping at all (despair);
By hoping that God will save us without our cooperation (presumption).

*We love God* when we delight in Him and desire Him above all things, with our whole heart, mind, and strength; and when we love our neighbor as ourselves.

We sin against the love of God by not keeping His Commandments.

*We adore God:*
By worshiping Him as the Lord and Creator of all things;
By praising Him;
By thanking Him for His graces;
By asking His help in prayer (petition); and
By offering Him satisfaction for sin (reparation).

The first Commandment of God also forbids: *Idolatry, Superstition,* and *Sacrilege.*

By *Idolatry* we mean paying to creatures the honor and adoration we owe to God.
The Bible tells us that the Israelites worshiped a golden calf. (*Ex.* 32).

By *Superstition* we mean ascribing to certain creatures a strange, hidden power that God has not given to them.

By a *Sacrilege* we mean misusing anything that is blessed or consecrated; that is, holy things, places, or persons.

## THE VENERATION OF THE SAINTS

*God wishes us to venerate or honor the Saints:*
Because they are His special friends;
Because they are glorified in Heaven with Him; and
Because they are our spiritual benefactors.

By *Saints* we mean those who have led a holy life, and are now happy with God in Heaven.

*We venerate the Saints:*
By imitating their virtues;
By celebrating their feasts;
By dedicating churches in their honor;
By honoring their statues, pictures, and relics; and
By asking them to pray for us.

*We should especially venerate the Blessed Virgin Mary:*
Because she is the Mother of God;
Because Jesus made her our spiritual Mother (*John* 19:26-27);
Because she is the Queen of Heaven and earth; and
Because her prayers are most powerful. (*John* 2).
*"For behold from henceforth all generations shall call me blessed."* (*Luke* 1:48).

We honor the *pictures* and *statues* of Jesus Christ and the Saints, but we do not pray to them.
We honor them as we honor the statues and pictures of great statesmen and heroes, and because they help us to pray with greater devotion.

We also honor the relics of Jesus Christ and the Saints.
By a *relic* we mean either the remains of the Saints or any object that has been closely connected with them or Christ.

We honor the relics of Jesus Christ because of their closeness to Him.

The chief relics of Christ are: His Cross, Tunic, Winding-sheet, and the Veil of Veronica.

*We honor the remains of the Saints:*
Because their bodies were in an exalted degree the
    temples of the Holy Ghost; and
Because they will rise in great glory on the Last Day.

### THE INVOCATION OF THE SAINTS

By *Invocation of the Saints* we mean asking them to intercede for us with God by their prayers.

The first Commandment of God does not forbid us to pray to the Saints.

When we pray to God, we ask Him to help us by His Almighty power.

When we pray to the Saints, we ask them to help us by their prayers.

*"And the smoke of the incense of the prayers of the Saints ascended up before God from the hand of the Angel." (Apoc. 8:4).*

We pray to the Saints because, being the special friends of God, they can obtain favors for us from Him.

## THE SHRINE OF THE BLESSED VIRGIN
## AT LOURDES, FRANCE

The Shrine at Lourdes is a plain proof that God grants the prayers of His Saints, and most especially of the Virgin Mary. Thousands of people have been miraculously cured at this far-famed Shrine.

## THE SECOND COMMANDMENT OF GOD

The second Commandment of God is: *Thou shalt not take the name of the Lord thy God in vain.*

The second Commandment forbids all profanation of the Holy Name of God.

*We profane or dishonor the Name of God:*
By pronouncing it irreverently;
By cursing;
By blaspheming;
By sinful swearing; and
By breaking a vow.

We pronounce the name of God *irreverently* whenever we say it carelessly or with disrespect.

By *cursing* we mean wishing evil to one's self or others.

By *blasphemy* we mean using insulting language against God, the Saints, or holy things.

To *swear* or *take an oath* means to call God to witness that we are speaking the truth, or that we intend to do what we promise.

*We swear sinfully:*
When we swear falsely;
When we swear without necessity; and
When we swear to do evil.
To swear falsely, especially in court, is perjury and is a mortal sin.

A *Vow* is a promise freely made to God by which we bind ourselves, under penalty of sin, to do something that is pleasing to Him.
The three great vows of religion are: *Poverty, Chastity,* and *Obedience.*

## PETER'S DENIAL

*"Then he began to curse and to swear that he knew not the man." (Matt. 26:74).*

## THE THIRD COMMANDMENT OF GOD

The third Commandment of God is: *Remember that thou keep holy the Sabbath Day.*

The Sabbath Day is Saturday, the seventh day of the week.
It is the day which was kept holy in the Old Testament.

In the New Testament, Sunday and not the Sabbath is kept holy.
This change was made by the Apostles.

*The Church commands us to keep Sunday instead of the Sabbath Day holy:*
Because Jesus Christ arose from the tomb on a Sunday; and
Because the Holy Ghost descended upon the Apostles on that day.

*We keep Sunday holy:*
By hearing Mass; and
By not doing servile work.

*We are obliged to hear Mass on Sunday:*
Because the first Commandment of the Church commands this; and
Because the Holy Sacrifice of the Mass is the highest act of worship that can be offered to God.

Servile works are those which are commonly performed by servants, day-laborers, and trades-people.
They are lawful on Sunday when the honor of God, the good of neighbor, or necessity requires them.

*"Remember that thou keep holy the Sabbath Day." (Ex. 20:8).*

## THE FOURTH COMMANDMENT OF GOD

The fourth Commandment of God is: *Honor thy father and thy mother.*

Children must honor father and mother, because they take the place of God for them, and are, next to Him, their greatest benefactors.

*Children honor father and mother:*
By loving them;
By obeying them; and
By praying for them.

*Children sin against the fourth Commandment:*
By treating their parents harshly; and
By not obeying them.

Children who honor their parents may expect the blessing of God in this life, and eternal happiness in the next.
*"Honor thy father and thy mother, that thou mayest be longlived upon the land." (Ex.* 20:12).

Children who do not honor their parents may expect the curse of God in this life, and His punishment in the life to come.
*"He that curseth his father, or mother, shall die the death." (Ex.* 21:17).

The fourth Commandment of God not only obliges children to honor father and mother, but also their superiors.

Our superiors are our bishop, parish priest, teachers, employers, and civil authorities.
We are obliged to honor and obey them, because their authority comes from God and because they take His place.

The fourth Commandment of God does not oblige children to obey their parents or superiors when they command them to commit sin.

## 1. JESUS WAS OBEDIENT TO MARY AND JOSEPH

*"And He went down with them, and came to Nazareth, and was subject to them." (Luke 2:51).*

**2.** Tobias curing his father's blindness. (*Tob.* 11:5-13).

**3.** Jesus consoles His dying foster-father Joseph.

## THE FIFTH COMMANDMENT OF GOD

The fifth Commandment of God is: *Thou shalt not kill.*

The fifth Commandment of God forbids us to injure our neighbor or ourselves in body and in soul.

*We injure our neighbor in body:*
By taking his life (homicide, murder);
By shortening his life; and
By striking or wounding him.

We injure our neighbor in soul by giving him scandal.

*Scandal* means to do evil in the presence of others so as to lead them into sin.
*"Woe to the world because of scandals. For it must needs be that scandals come: but nevertheless woe to that man by whom the scandal cometh."* (*Matt.* 18:7).

Whenever we have injured our neighbor in body or soul, we are bound in conscience to try to make good the evil we have done.

*We sin against our own life:*
By taking it (suicide);
By endangering it without necessity; and
By injuring our health.

*We injure our health:*
By neglecting it;
By violent anger; and
By intemperance in eating or drinking.

*We sin in thought against the fifth Commandment:*
By hating our neighbor;
By desiring revenge; and
By wishing him death or evil.
*"Whosoever hateth his brother is a murderer."* (*1 Jn.* 3:15).

*"And when they were in the field, Cain rose up against his brother Abel, and slew him."* (Gen. 4:8).

## THE SIXTH COMMANDMENT OF GOD

The sixth Commandment of God is: *Thou shalt not commit adultery.*

The sixth Commandment of God forbids all sins against purity and modesty.
*"Be ye holy, because I the Lord your God am holy."* (*Lev.* 19:2).
*"Know you not that you are the temples of God, and that the Spirit of God dwelleth in you?"* (*1 Cor.* 3:16).

*We sin against the sixth Commandment of God:*
By impure thoughts and desires;
By impure words or conversation;
By impure looks;
By reading impure books; and
By impure actions.

We should be always on our guard against sins of impurity, because none are more shameful and none more severely punished by God.
God punished the people of Noah's time with a flood for sins of impurity. (*Gen.* 6:7).
He destroyed the shameful cities of Sodom and Gomorrha with brimstone and fire. (*Gen.* 19).

*To avoid sins of impurity we should:*
Say our prayers regularly;
Keep away from bad company;
Receive the Sacraments often;
Pray to God, the Blessed Virgin Mary, and our Guardian Angel in times of temptation, and
Remember that God sees everything.

*"Blessed are the clean of heart: for they shall see God."* (*Matt.* 5:8).

**GOD SENT THE DELUGE AS A PUNISHMENT
FOR SINS OF IMPURITY.** (*Gen.* 6).

## THE SEVENTH COMMANDMENT OF GOD

The seventh Commandment of God is: *Thou shalt not steal.*

*To steal* means to take or keep unjustly what belongs to another.

The seventh Commandment obliges us to respect the property of our neighbor.

By *property* we mean those things which belong to a person.

*We injure our neighbor in his property:*
By stealing (theft, robbery);
By cheating;
By not restoring things found to the owner;
By not paying our debts; and
By damaging our neighbor's goods.

It is a sin for children to steal from their parents, brothers, or sisters.

It is a sin to tell others to steal or to help them in stealing.

When we have injured our neighbor in his property by stealing or in any other way, we are bound in conscience to make restitution; that is, make good the damage we have done.

*"I have been young, and now am old; and I have not seen the just forsaken."* (*Ps.* 36:25).

THE ANGEL RAPHAEL CLAIMING BACK FROM
GABELUS THE SUM OF MONEY WHICH THE ELDER
TOBIAS HAD LENT HIM. (*Tob.* 9:3-6).

## THE EIGHTH COMMANDMENT OF GOD

The eighth Commandment of God is: *Thou shalt not bear false witness against thy neighbor.*

*We commit sin against the eighth Commandment:*
When we tell a lie; and
When we injure our neighbor's good name.

By a *Lie* we mean saying what is not true, with the intention of deceiving our neighbor.
*"Lying lips are an abomination to the Lord."* (*Prov.* 12:22).

We injure our neighbor's good name by *Slander* and *Detraction.*

*Slander* is falsely accusing our neighbor of something evil.

*Detraction* is telling the hidden faults of our neighbor without necessity.

We sin in thought against our neighbor's good name by *False Suspicion* and *Rash Judgment.*

*False Suspicion* is surmising evil of our neighbor without good reasons.

*Rash Judgment* is believing evil of our neighbor without good reasons.
*"Judge not, and you shall not be judged."* (*Luke* 6:37).

Whenever we have injured the good name of our neighbor, we are bound in conscience to repair the injury.

**"AND THE CHIEF PRIESTS ACCUSED HIM
IN MANY THINGS."** (*Mark* 15:3).

## THE NINTH COMMANDMENT OF GOD

The ninth Commandment of God is: *Thou shalt not covet thy neighbor's wife.*

The ninth Commandment of God forbids impure thoughts and desires, especially in regard to married persons.

*"Evil thoughts are an abomination to the Lord."* (*Prov.* 15:26).

Impure thoughts and desires are not sinful if we try to banish them from our mind.

When we are tempted with impure thoughts and desires we should especially pray to God, the Blessed Virgin Mary, and our Guardian Angel.

We should remember that God knows our most secret thoughts and desires.

*"Blessed are the clean of heart: for they shall see God."* (*Matt.* 5:8).

Note: See Sixth Commandment of God. (p. 90).

Impure thoughts and desires lead to impure deeds. The woman in the picture was guilty of these sins. Jesus saved her from the scribes and Pharisees, who sought to stone her, and said to her: *"Go, and now sin no more."* (*John* 8:3-11).

## THE TENTH COMMANDMENT OF GOD

The tenth Commandment of God is: *Thou shalt not covet thy neighbor's goods.*

To *covet* means *"to desire."*

The tenth Commandment of God forbids us to desire our neighbor's goods.

Before God the intention to steal from our neighbor is just as wicked as the deed itself.

The tenth Commandment of God also forbids the sins of *envy* and *discontent.*

By *Envy* we mean begrudging our neighbor his good fortune and success.

By *Discontent* we mean complaining that our lot in life is worse than that of our neighbor.

*"Seek ye first the Kingdom of God and His Justice, and all these things shall be added unto you." (Luke* 12:31).

*"For the desire of money is the root of all evils; which some coveting have erred from the faith, and have entangled themselves in many sorrows." (1 Tim.* 6:10).

The treasures of the Temple were coveted by Seleucus, king of Asia. He ordered Heliodorus, the general of his army, to seize them. When the general arrived at the Temple a mysterious horse and rider struck him down, while two Angels of the Lord beat him unceasingly. (*2 Mach.* 3).

## THE CHILD JESUS IN THE TEMPLE

*"Do not think that I am come to destroy the law...I am not come to destroy, but to fulfill." (Matt. 5:17).*

*"And He went down with them, and came to Nazareth, and was subject to them." (Luke 2:51).*

## THE SIX COMMANDMENTS OF THE CHURCH

*The six Commandments of the Church are:*

1. To rest from servile work and to hear Mass on Sundays and Holydays of obligation.

2. To fast and abstain on the days appointed.

3. To confess our sins at least once a year.

4. To receive Holy Communion at least once a year and that at Easter or thereabouts. (see p. 108.)

5. To contribute to the support of the Church and parish priest.

6. Not to marry contrary to the laws of the Church, and not to belong to forbidden societies.

Jesus Christ gave His Church the power and authority to make laws when He said to His Apostles:
*"As the Father hath sent Me, I also send you."* (*John* 20:21).
*"Amen I say to you, whatsoever you shall bind upon earth, shall be bound also in Heaven."* (*Matt.* 18:18).
*"He that heareth you, heareth Me; and he that despiseth you, despiseth Me."* (*Luke* 10:16).

We are bound to keep the Commandments of the Church, because obedience to Her is obedience to Jesus Christ.

## THE FIRST COMMANDMENT OF THE CHURCH

The first Commandment of the Church is: *To rest from servile work and to hear Mass on Sundays and Holydays of obligation.*

The first Commandment of the Church binds all Catholics who have reached the age of reason.

*The Holydays of obligation in the United States are:*
1. The Circumcision of Our Lord. January 1.
2. The Ascension of Our Lord. Forty days after Easter.
3. The Assumption of the Blessed Virgin Mary. August 15.
4. All Saints' Day. November 1.
5. The Immaculate Conception of the Blessed Virgin Mary. December 8.
6. Christmas. December 25.

The Holydays of obligation were instituted by the Church to recall to our mind the great mysteries of our holy religion.

*We sin against the first Commandment of the Church:*
By missing Mass through our own fault on Sundays and Holydays of obligation;
By not hearing all of the Mass;
By being wilfully distracted during the Mass or sermon; and
By doing unnecessary work on these days.
*"The Lord is in His Holy Temple; let all the earth keep silence before Him." (Hab. 2:20).*

Those who must work on Sundays and Holydays of obligation are not excused from hearing Mass, if it is possible for them to attend.

## THE HOLY SACRIFICE OF THE MASS

*"From the rising of the sun even to the going down, My name is great among the Gentiles, and in every place there is sacrifice, and there is offered to My name a clean oblation."* (Mal. 1:11).

## THE SECOND COMMANDMENT OF THE CHURCH

The second Commandment of the Church is: *To fast and abstain on the days appointed.*

### FASTING

By Fasting the Church means taking but one full meal a day. [Two small meatless meals, sufficient to maintain strength and together not equalling the full meal, are also allowed. Eating between meals is not permitted, though liquids between meals, including milk and fruit juice, are permitted.]

Our Lord fasted forty days in the desert. Moses and Elias also fasted forty days.

All Catholics who have completed the age of twenty-one are obliged to fast, unless excused by some just cause.

*The Church excuses from Fasting:*
The sick and convalescent; those who do hard work; those who are very poor; those who have attained the age of fifty-nine; and those who have obtained a dispensation.

*The Fast-days of the Church are:*\*
The week-days of Lent (Monday-Saturday);
The vigils of Pentecost, Assumption, All Saints' Day and Christmas, plus the Ember days.

The Ember days, traditionally, are three in number: Wednesday, Friday and Saturday. They appear four times a year, at the beginning of each season.

*"Be converted to Me with all your heart, in fasting, and in weeping, and in mourning."* (*Joel* 2:12).

\*The days of fast are now only two: Ash Wednesday and Good Friday.—*Editor*, 1993.

**CHRIST FASTED FORTY DAYS AND FORTY NIGHTS
IN THE DESERT. (*Matt.* 4:2).**

### ABSTINENCE

By *Abstinence* we mean not to eat flesh-meat on the days appointed by the Church.

The Bible tells us that the Israelites were commanded by God to abstain from certain flesh-meats. (*Lev.* 11).

Every Catholic who has reached the age of reason* is obliged to abstain from flesh-meats on the days appointed, unless excused by some just cause.

*The days of Abstinence for Catholics in the United States are:**
All Fridays of the year; and
All Fast-days of the Church, unless a dispensation is granted by ecclesiastical authority.

---

*The days of abstinence are now only: Ash Wednesday and all Fridays of the year (except solemnities); outside of Lent some other penance may be substituted for abstinence. The obligation of abstinence *now* binds from age 14. (The age of reason is normally 7 years old, at the latest.)—*Editor,* 1993.

The Church has appointed Friday as a day of Abstinence in memory of the death of the world's Redeemer.

*The Church commands us to fast and abstain:*
To help us follow the example of Jesus Christ;
To help us do penance for our sins; and
To help us mortify our evil passions.

### THE THIRD COMMANDMENT OF THE CHURCH

The third Commandment of the Church is: *To confess our sins at least once a year.*

All Catholics who have reached the age of reason are bound by the third Commandment of the Church.

We sin against the third Commandment of the Church when we neglect to confess our sins at least once a year [if we have a mortal sin to confess].

It is not enough for us to confess our sins once a year. This is the least the Church expects of us.
If we wish to lead a good and holy life, we must confess often.
*"For what doth it profit a man, if he gain the whole world, and suffer the loss of his own soul?"* (*Matt.* 16:26).

## CONFESSION

*"Whose sins you shall forgive, they are forgiven them; and
whose sins you shall retain, they are retained." (John 20:23).*

## THE FOURTH COMMANDMENT OF THE CHURCH

The fourth Commandment of the Church is: *To receive Holy Communion at least once a year, and that at Easter or thereabouts.*

The fourth Commandment of the Church binds all Catholics who have reached the age of reason and have been admitted to Holy Communion.

In most of the dioceses in the United States, the Easter time begins with the first Sunday of Lent and closes with Trinity Sunday.

If it is possible, the Easter Communion should be made in the parish church.

Christian burial can be refused to those who have neglected to fulfill this Commandment.

*"Amen, Amen I say unto you: except you eat the Flesh of the Son of Man, and drink His Blood, you shall not have life in you." (John 6:54).*

## HOLY COMMUNION

*"I am the Living Bread which came down from Heaven.
"If any man eat of this Bread, he shall live forever."* (*John*
6:51, 52.)

### THE FIFTH COMMANDMENT OF THE CHURCH

The fifth Commandment of the Church is: *To contribute to the support of the Church and the parish priest.*

In the Old Testament the Jews were commanded by God to give one-tenth of their possessions and earnings to the Temple. (*Ex.* 22:29 23:16, 19).

Jesus Christ praised a Jewish widow one day for giving all that she had to the treasury of the Temple. (*Mark* 12:42, 43).

Both the Church and the parish priest cannot subsist without support from the laity.
*"So also the Lord ordained that they who preach the Gospel, should live by the Gospel."* (*1 Cor.* 9:14).
*"The laborer is worthy of his hire."* (*Luke* 10:7).

Every Catholic wage-earner, therefore, is bound by this Commandment to contribute to the support of the Church and the parish priest, according to his means.

## THE WIDOW'S MITE

*"Amen I say to you, this poor widow hath cast in more than all they who have cast into the treasury. For all they did cast in of their abundance; but she of her want cast in all she had."* (*Mark* 12:43, 44).

## THE SIXTH COMMANDMENT OF THE CHURCH

The sixth Commandment of the Church is: *Not to marry contrary to the laws of the Church, and not to belong to forbidden societies.*

*Not to marry contrary to the laws of the Church means that Catholics are forbidden:*
To marry within the third degree of kindred;
To marry a non-Catholic;
To marry before anyone but the parish priest and two Catholic witnesses.

*Not to marry within the third degree of kindred* means that Catholics are forbidden to marry relatives as far as and including second cousins.

*Not to marry a non-Catholic* means that the Church disapproves of mixed marriages, because there is a great danger for the Catholic party of losing the Faith.

*Not to marry before anyone but the parish priest and two Catholic witnesses means:*
That the parish priest has the right to officiate at the marriages of his parishioners; and
That the laws of the Church require the presence of two witnesses.

Catholics are not married before God and the Church if they attempt marriage before a judge or non-Catholic minister.

By being married at a Nuptial Mass, Catholics show a great reverence for the Sacrament of Matrimony, and gain rich graces for their wedded life.

*Not to belong to forbidden societies* means that Catholics are forbidden to become members of the Masons, Odd Fellows, and Knights of Pythias.

*The Church forbids her members to join these organizations:*
Because of their secrecy; and
Because they have a definite religious rite.

**HOW SACRED THE MARRIAGE OF JOSEPH AND MARY**

*"For we are the children of saints, and we must not be joined together like heathens that know not God." (Tob. 8:5).*

## THE PRACTICE OF CHRISTIAN VIRTUE

To be a true Christian it is not enough for us to keep the Commandments; we must also practice virtue.

By *Christian virtue* we mean the constant will and effort to do what is pleasing to God.

*There are two kinds of virtue:*
The Theological or divine virtues; and
The moral virtues.

The Theological or divine virtues are: Faith, Hope, and Charity.
They are called Theological or divine virtues because they have God for their immediate object.
They are placed into our soul when we are baptized.

The chief moral virtues are: Prudence, Justice, Fortitude, and Temperance.
They are called moral virtues because they bring our life into conformity with the moral law, regulating our conduct with regard to ourselves and our neighbor.
These four virtues are also called the four *Cardinal virtues*.

The four Cardinal virtues of Prudence, Justice, Fortitude and Temperance are divided into seven other moral virtues: Humility, Liberality, Chastity, Meekness, Temperance in Eating and Drinking, Brotherly Love, and Zeal.

### THE THEOLOGICAL OR DIVINE VIRTUES

The virtue of *Faith* leads us to believe in the existence of God, His divine perfections, and His revelations.
It is opposed to Infidelity.

## THE THEOLOGICAL VIRTUES OF FAITH, HOPE, AND CHARITY

1. Abraham's Faith in God. He was ready to sacrifice his son Isaac at God's command. (*Gen.* 22).

2. Moses in holy anger at the infidelity of the Israelites. (*Ex.* 32).

3. Job's hope in God was supreme, even in the midst of great trials and sufferings. (*Job* 2:10)

4. Realizing that he had betrayed the innocent blood of the Son of God, Judas *despaired*, and hanged himself. (*Matt.* 27:4, 5).

5. Jesus praising Mary, the sister of Martha, for her great love of God. (*Luke* 10:38-42).

6. When Pontius Pilate presented Jesus, scourged and crowned with thorns, the Jews showed the depth of their Hatred and Ingratitude by crying out: *"Crucify Him, crucify Him."* (*John* 19:4-6).

The virtue of *Hope* helps us to look to God for eternal salvation and the means to gain it.

It is opposed to Despair and Presumption.

The virtue of *Charity* moves us to love God, that is, to seek to please Him by doing His Holy Will.

It is opposed to Ingratitude and Hatred.

*We should often make acts of Faith, Hope, and Charity, especially*

When we are tempted against these three virtues;

When we are about to receive any of the Sacraments; and

When we are in danger of death.

### THE FOUR CARDINAL VIRTUES

The virtue of *Prudence* helps us not only to know and will what is good and right, but also to choose the proper means to do what is good and right.

It is opposed to Imprudence.

The virtue of *Justice* disposes us to render to our neighbor his rights.

It is opposed to Injustice.

The virtue of *Fortitude* gives us courage to suffer anything in the performance of our duties.

It is opposed to Cowardice.

The virtue of *Temperance* helps us to keep our inclinations and desires within the bounds of what is lawful.

It is opposed to Intemperance.

We should try very hard to practice the four Cardinal Virtues because they are the foundation of a true Christian life.

## PRUDENCE, JUSTICE, FORTITUDE, TEMPERANCE

1. Solomon's *prudent* judgment. (*3 Kgs.* 2).

2. The prophet Nathan was sent by God to David to chide him for his *Imprudence*. (*2 Kgs.* 12).

3. *"Render to Caesar the things that are Caesar's, and to God, the things that are God's."* (*Matt.* 22:21).

4. Joseph was *unjustly* sold to the Egyptians by his brothers. (*Gen.* 37).

5. The *Fortitude* of St. Stephen, the first Christian martyr. (*Acts* 7:57-59).

6. Peter *cowardly* denied his Lord. (*Matt.* 26:69-75).

7. The prophet Daniel was a man of *Temperance*. (*Dan.* 1:8).

8. The *intemperate* Baltasar. (*Dan.* 5).

## THE SEVEN MORAL VIRTUES

The moral virtues of Humility, Liberality, Chastity, Meekness, Temperance in Eating and Drinking, Brotherly Love, and Zeal are opposed to the Seven Capital Sins.

The seven *Capital Sins* are: Pride, Avarice, Lust, Anger, Gluttony, Envy, and Sloth.

They are called the seven Capital Sins because they are the chief sources of sin.

Humility is opposed to Pride:
*"Blessed are the poor in spirit: for theirs is the Kingdom of Heaven."* (*Matt.* 5:3).
*"God resisteth the proud, but to the humble He giveth grace."* (*1 Ptr.* 5:5).

Liberality is opposed to Avarice:
*"Blessed are the merciful: for they shall obtain mercy."* (*Matt.* 5:7).
*"The desire of money is the root of all evils."* (*1 Tim.* 6:10).

Chastity is opposed to Lust:
*"Blessed are the clean of heart: for they shall see God."* (*Matt.* 5:8).
*"Know you not, that you are the temple of God, and that the Spirit of God dwelleth in you?"* (*1 Cor.* 3:16).

Meekness is opposed to Anger:
*"Take up My yoke upon you, and learn of Me, because I am meek, and humble of heart; and you shall find rest to your souls."* (*Matt.* 11:29).
*"Let every man be swift to hear, but slow to speak, and slow to anger. For the anger of man worketh not the justice of God."* (*James* 1:19).

## HUMILITY, LIBERALITY, CHASTITY, MEEKNESS

1. The *humble* publican praying with downcast eyes. (*Luke* 18:10-14).

2. The *Pride* of Absalom led him to conspire against his father, David. (*2 Kgs.* 15 ff.).

3. The *Liberality* of the wise men from the East. (*Matt.* 2:11).

4. In *Avarice* Judas betrayed and sold his Master for thirty pieces of silver. (*Matt.* 26:14, 15).

5. "*Behold the Lamb of God, behold Him who taketh away the sin of the world.*" (*John* 1:29).

6. The Prodigal Son. (*Luke* 15:11-32).

7. The supreme *Meekness* of Jesus Christ. (*Mark* 15:16-20).

8. In *Anger* Saul attempts to nail David to the wall with his spear. (*1 Kgs.* 19:10).

Temperance in eating and drinking is opposed to Gluttony:

*"Whether you eat or drink, or whatsoever else you do, do all to the Glory of God."* (*1 Cor.* 10:31).

*"Take heed to yourselves, lest perhaps your hearts be overcharged with surfeiting and drunkenness, and the cares of this life."* (*Luke* 21:34).

Brotherly Love is opposed to Envy:

*"By this shall all men know that you are My disciples, if you have love one for another."* (*John* 13:35).

*"By the envy of the devil, death came into the world."* (*Wis.* 2:24).

Zeal is opposed to Sloth:

*"Not every one that saith to Me, Lord, Lord, shall enter into the Kingdom of Heaven: but he that doth the will of My Father Who is in Heaven, he shall enter into the Kingdom of Heaven."* (*Matt.* 7:21).

*"Every tree that bringeth not forth good fruit, shall be cut down, and shall be cast into the fire."* (*Matt.* 7:19).

Some of the rewards that God will mete out to those who practice Christian virtue are to be found in the Eight Beatitudes.

Jesus Christ proclaimed the Eight Beatitudes in His Sermon on the Mount. (*Matt.* 5, 6, 7).

## TEMPERANCE IN EATING AND DRINKING, BROTHERLY LOVE, AND ZEAL

1. The prophet Daniel was a man of *Temperance*. (*Dan.* 1:8).

2. The *Intemperance* of Baltasar. (*Dan.* 5).

3. The *Brotherly Love* of Joseph of Egypt. (*Gen.* 44:1).

4. The *Envy* of Cain. (*Gen.* 4:5).

5. Noemi and Ruth. The *Zeal* of Ruth. She gathered up the ears of corn that escaped the hands of the reapers. (*Ruth* 2:2-3).

6. Moses in holy anger over the *Sloth* of the Israelites. (*Ex.* 32).

### JESUS CHRIST PROCLAIMING
### THE EIGHT BEATITUDES. (*Matt.* 5).

### THE EIGHT BEATITUDES

1. Blessed are the poor in spirit: for theirs is the Kingdom of Heaven.

2. Blessed are the meek: for they shall possess the land.

3. Blessed are they that mourn: for they shall be comforted.

4. Blessed are they that hunger and thirst after Justice: for they shall have their fill.

5. Blessed are the merciful: for they shall obtain mercy.

6. Blessed are the clean of heart: for they shall see God.

7. Blessed are the peacemakers: for they shall be called the children of God.

8. Blessed are they that suffer persecution for justice' sake: for theirs is the Kingdom of Heaven. (*Matt.* 5:3-10).

## CHRISTIAN PERFECTION

Christian Perfection consists in the love of God above all things, and in the love of neighbor as ourselves.

*"But above all these things have Charity, which is the bond of perfection." (Col.* 3:14).

The best way to practice Christian Perfection is to imitate Jesus Christ.

*"If thou wilt be perfect, go sell what thou hast, and give to the poor, and thou shalt have treasure in Heaven: and come follow Me." (Matt.* 19:21).

The three great means for attaining Christian Perfection are: *Voluntary Poverty, Perpetual Chastity,* and *Voluntary Obedience.*

They are also called the Evangelical Counsels.

The main purpose of the Religious Life is to practice these Evangelical Counsels in a high degree.

The practice of Christian Perfection is open to all Christians.

*"Be you therefore perfect, as also your Heavenly Father is perfect." (Matt.* 5:48).

## FIVE GREAT FOUNDERS OF RELIGIOUS ORDERS

St. Francis.              St. Benedict.
St. Dominic.        St. Alphonsus.         St. Ignatius.

## SIN

Sin is a willful breaking of the Law of God, that is, of the ten Commandments and the Commandments of the Church.

Sin is the greatest evil in the world, because by it we offend God, and can lose our immortal soul.
*"What doth it profit a man, if he gain the whole world, and suffer the loss of his own soul?"* (*Matt.* 16:26).

*Sin may be committed in five different ways:*
By thoughts;
By desires;
By words;
By looks; and
By actions.

The first sin of man was committed by Adam and Eve. This sin is called Original Sin.

*There are two kinds of sin:*
Mortal sin and venial sin, or
Big sins and little sins.

*Big sins are called mortal sins:*
Because they destroy the supernatural life of the soul, which is Sanctifying Grace; and
Because they bring the danger of everlasting death upon it.

*To make a sin* MORTAL, *three things are required:*
A serious matter;
Sufficient reflection of the mind; and
Full consent of the will.

We commit a *mortal* sin when we willfully and knowingly break the Commandments in a serious matter.

*We commit a* VENIAL SIN:
When we break the Commandments in a small matter; or
When we break them in a serious matter but without sufficient reflection of the mind and full consent of the will.

*The chief results of mortal sin are:*
It robs us of Sanctifying Grace;
It deprives us of all Heavenly merits; and
It places us in danger of everlasting death.
*"Thou hast the name of being alive: and thou art dead." (Apoc.* 3:1).

*The chief results of venial sin are:*
It lessens the love of God in our heart;
It makes us less worthy of His graces;
It weakens our will-power; and
It gradually leads to mortal sin.
*"He that contemneth* [that is, *scorns] small things, shall fall by little and little." (Ecclus.* 19:1).

The chief sources of sin are: *Pride, Avarice, Lust, Anger, Gluttony, Envy,* and *Sloth.*
They are called the seven Capital Sins.
Temptations and occasions of sin lead us into sin.

*Temptations* are thoughts and suggestions.
*Occasions of sin* are persons, places, or things.
*"He that loveth danger shall perish in it." (Ecclus.* 3:27).

**JESUS IN GETHSEMANE**

*"And He was withdrawn away from them a stone's cast; and kneeling down, He prayed.*

*"Saying: Father, if Thou wilt, remove this chalice from Me: but yet not My will, but Thine be done." (Luke 22:41, 42).*

# PART III

*The third part of this book teaches us the means given to us by God to* RECEIVE, PRESERVE *and* INCREASE *the divine life in our souls.*

**"IT IS CONSUMMATED."** (*John* 19:30).

## THE REDEMPTION

God did not abandon man after his fall into sin, but from the beginning promised him a Redeemer. (*Gen.* 3:15).

This Redeemer was to satisfy for man's sin, and reopen to him the gates of Heaven.

The Prophets foretold the coming of the Redeemer, and many things about His life, death, and triumph.

The promised Redeemer is Jesus Christ the Son of God, Who was born in Bethlehem and was crucified on Mount Calvary.

The Son of God became man to *redeem* us, that is, to suffer and die for our sins.
*"Thou shalt call His name Jesus, for He shall save His people from their sins."* (*Matt.* 1:21).

*By the sin of Adam and Eve:*
God was infinitely offended;
Sanctifying Grace was lost to man; and
The gates of Heaven were closed.

*By the merits of Jesus Christ, and especially by His death upon the Cross:*
The Justice of God was perfectly satisfied;
Sanctifying Grace was restored to man; and
The gates of Heaven were reopened.

The promised Redeemer not only satisfied for the sin of Adam and Eve, but also for the sins of the whole world.
*"He is the propitiation for our sins; and not for ours only, but also for those of the whole world."* (*1 Jn.* 2:2).

This satisfaction for the sin of Adam and Eve, and for the sins of the whole world, was given to God's infinite Justice by a sacrifice of infinite value, which was offered by the infinite Son of God.
By the Sacrifice of the Cross, Jesus Christ, the infinite Son of God, paid to the Heavenly Father man's infinite debt of sin.

The sacrifice of the Cross is the sacrifice of the New Testament, perpetuated in the Holy Sacrifice of the Mass.

## THE HOLY SACRIFICE OF THE MASS

The Holy Sacrifice of the Mass is the constant renewal of the Sacrifice of the Cross.

To offer sacrifice means to offer God a visible gift, whole and entire.

*For a sacrifice three things are required:*
A visible gift;
A priest who offers it to God; and
An altar on which it is offered.

The perfect Sacrifice of all time is the infinite Sacrifice of the Cross, in which Jesus Christ the Son of God offered Himself to His Heavenly Father for the sins of the whole world.
He was the visible gift;
He was also the priest who offered; and
His Cross was the altar.

In the Sacrifice of the Cross, Jesus Christ offered Himself in a bloody manner.
In the Sacrifice of the Mass, He offers Himself in an unbloody manner.

Jesus Christ instituted the Sacrifice of the Mass at the Last Supper, in the presence of His twelve Apostles. (*Matt.* 26:26-28).

Jesus Christ made the Sacrifice of the Mass identical with the Sacrifice of the Cross when He gave His Body and Blood to His Apostles and said to them:
*"This is My Body, which shall be delivered for you."* (*1 Cor.* 11:24).
*"This is My Blood of the New Testament, which shall be shed for many."* (*Mark* 14:24).
*"Do this for a commemoration of Me."* (*Luke* 22:19).

## THE LAST SUPPER

"*Whilst they were at supper, Jesus took bread, and blessed, and broke: and gave to His disciples, and said: Take ye, and eat.* THIS IS MY BODY.

"*And taking the chalice, He gave thanks, and gave to them, saying: Drink ye all of this.*

"*FOR THIS IS MY BLOOD OF THE NEW TESTAMENT, which shall be shed for many unto the remission of sins.*" (*Matt.* 26:26-28).

"*Do this for a commemoration of Me.*" (*Luke* 22:19).

Jesus Christ gave His Apostles and their successors, the bishops and priests of the Catholic Church, the power to change bread and wine into His Body and Blood when He said:

*"Do this for a commemoration of Me." (Luke* 22:19).

Sacrifices were offered to God from the beginning of the world.

The sacrifices of the Old Testament were types and figures of the Infinite Sacrifice of the New Testament.

The prophet Malachias foretold the Sacrifice of the Mass.

*"From the rising of the sun even to the going down, My name is great among the Gentiles; and in every place there is sacrifice, and there is offered to My name a clean oblation." (Mal.* 1:11).

The Bible tells us that the Apostles offered the Sacrifice of the Mass.

*"The Chalice of Benediction, which we bless, is it not the communion of the Blood of Christ? And the Bread, which we break, is it not the partaking of the Body of the Lord?" (1 Cor.* 10:16).

The Bible also tells us that the Apostles conferred the power to offer the Sacrifice of the Mass upon their successors.

*"And when they had ordained to them priests in every church, and had prayed with fasting, they commended them to the Lord, in Whom they believed." (Acts* 14:22).

1. The sacrifice of Noah was a sacrifice of thanksgiving to God. (*Gen.* 8:20, 21).

2. Abraham was ready to sacrifice his son Isaac in obedience to God's command. (*Gen.* 22).

3. Melchisedech, the king of Salem and a priest of the Most High God, offered bread and wine. (*Gen.* 14:18).

4. The institution of the Holy Sacrifice of the Mass. (*Luke* 22:19, 20.)

The Bishops and priests of the Catholic Church have the power to offer the Sacrifice of the Mass because they are the lawful successors of the Apostles.

*The principal parts of the Holy Sacrifice of the Mass are:*

The Offertory;
The Consecration; and
The Communion.

At the *Offertory* the priest offers bread and wine to God.

At the *Consecration* he changes bread and wine into the Body and Blood of Jesus Christ.

At the *Communion* the priest and the people receive the Body and Blood of Jesus Christ.

*The Holy Sacrifice of the Mass is offered for four great ends:*

As a Sacrifice of Praise;
As a Sacrifice of Thanksgiving;
As a Sacrifice of Atonement; and
As a Sacrifice of Prayer (that is, of Petition).

*Those who are especially benefited by the Holy Sacrifice of the Mass are:*

The priest who offers it;
Those who assist at it with devotion; and
Those for whom it is offered.

## THE HOLY SACRIFICE OF THE MASS

We should assist at the Holy Sacrifice of the Mass with great piety and devotion, because Jesus Christ becomes really and truly present on the altar by the *consecrating Power* of the priest.

## GRACE

*The chief results of the Redemption are:*
The satisfaction of the Justice of God;
The reopening of Heaven; and
The regaining of Grace.
*"Being justified freely by His Grace, through the Redemption that is in Christ Jesus." (Rom.* 3:24).

*Grace* is an interior supernatural free gift, which God confers upon the *soul,* through the merits of Jesus Christ, for our salvation.
The merits of Jesus Christ are His life, works, sufferings, and death.

Grace is a supernatural free gift.
It is a *supernatural gift,* because God confers it upon us for our salvation.
It is a *free gift,* because He gives it to us without any claim on our part.
Since Grace is a free gift of God, He is free to give more and greater Graces to some than to others.

The Bible tells us that God gives all men sufficient Grace to be saved.
*"Who will have all men to be saved, and to come to the knowledge of the truth." (1 Tim.* 2:4).

Because we have a free will, we can co-operate with Grace or reject it.

Those who co-operate with Grace are like the man of the parable who received five talents and used them well.
To him the Lord said: *"Well done, good and faithful servant, because thou hast been faithful over a few things, I will place thee over many things." (Matt.* 25:21).

1. One of the chief results of the Redemption is the regaining of Grace for men. (*Rom.* 3:24).

2. The Immaculate Virgin Mary was full of Grace. (*Luke* 1:28).

3. God sows the seeds of Grace like the sower of the parable; some fall upon stony ground and among thorns, and some upon good ground. (*Matt.* 13).

4. Those who co-operate with the Grace of God hearken to the knocks of the Master on the door of their heart. Those who reject the Grace of God disregard His knocks. (*Apoc.* 3:20).

Those who reject Grace are like the man of the parable who received one talent and did not use it.

Of him the Lord said: *"Take ye away therefore the talent from him, and give it to him that hath ten talents."* (*Matt.* 25:28).

*There are two kinds of Grace:*
Actual Grace; and
Sanctifying Grace.

## ACTUAL GRACE

*Actual Grace* is that help from God which enlightens our reason and moves our will to do good and to avoid evil.

The conversion of St. Paul on his journey to Damascus, to persecute the Christians there, is an inspiring example of Actual Grace.

A light from Heaven enlightened his mind, and the voice of Jesus Christ in the clouds moved his will.

He co-operated with this Grace, was converted, and became the great Apostle of the Gentiles. (*Acts* 9).

Actual Grace is so necessary to us that without it we cannot begin, continue, or accomplish the least thing towards our eternal salvation.

*"Without Me you can do nothing."* (*John* 15:5).

Actual Grace comes to us through various channels: the Sacraments, Attendance at the Holy Sacrifice of the Mass, Prayer, Sermons, Good Works, Sickness, and the Good Example of Others.

"I CAN DO ALL THINGS IN HIM WHO
STRENGTHENETH ME." (*Phil.* 4:13).

1. The priest is like the angels on the ladder of Jacob. By administering the Sacraments he brings the Grace of God to man, and returns the works of man to God. (*Gen.* 28:12).

2. On Pentecost Day the Apostles received very special Graces from God. They were filled with the Holy Ghost and His Gifts. (*Acts* 2).

3. Jesus Christ gave the Grace of faith to the Samaritan woman and her fellowmen. (*John* 4).

4. Peter walked miraculously upon the sea but doubted the power of God and began to sink. (*Matt.* 14:28, 29, 30).

5. The Grace of God sustained St. Stephen in his martyrdom. (*Acts* 7:58).

6. The Conversion of St. Paul. (*Acts* 9).

## SANCTIFYING GRACE

*Sanctifying Grace* is an unmerited gift of the Holy Ghost, whereby we become children of God and heirs of Heaven.

Sanctifying Grace is the supernatural life, beauty, and brightness conferred on our soul by the presence of the Holy Ghost.

It makes our soul the object of the special love and friendship of God.

*"Know you not, that you are the Temple of God, and that the Spirit of God dwelleth in you?"* (*1 Cor.* 3:16).

Without Sanctifying Grace, we cannot merit anything for Heaven.

*"Abide in Me, and I in you. As the branch cannot bear fruit of itself, unless it abide in the vine, so neither can you, unless you abide in Me."* (*John* 15:4).

Deeds or works that are performed in the state of Sanctifying Grace are meritorious; that is, they have an eternal value in the kingdom of Heaven.

*"Every good tree bringeth forth good fruit, and the evil tree bringeth forth evil fruit."* (*Matt.* 7:17).

The Blessed Virgin Mary enjoyed a fullness of Sanctifying Grace.

*"And the Angel being come in, said unto her: Hail, full of Grace, the Lord is with thee."* (*Luke* 1:28).

The Grace of Perseverance is a special divine gift, whereby we are helped to continue in the service of God until death.

*"Be thou faithful unto death: and I will give thee the crown of life."* (*Apoc.* 2:10).

## GOOD WORKS

*Good Works are deeds:*
Pleasing to God; and
Meritorious for Heaven.

Good Works are necessary for salvation.
*"Faith, if it have not works, is dead in itself."* (*James* 2:26).
*"Every tree therefore that doth not yield good fruit, shall be cut down, and cast into the fire."* (*Matt.* 3:10).

To be pleasing to God and meritorious for Heaven, our deeds must be performed in the state of Sanctifying Grace and with the good intention.
*"As the branch cannot bear fruit of itself unless it abide in the vine, so neither can you, unless you abide in Me."* (*John* 15:4).

The Bible especially recommends the following Good Works: Prayer, Fasting, and Alms-deeds.
*"Prayer is good with fasting and alms more than to lay up treasures of gold."* (*Tob.* 12:8).

A very important thing to remember about Good Works is the *Good Intention.*
The *Good Intention* is the desire to serve God and honor Him.
We may briefly form a Good Intention by saying: *"All to the greater honor and glory of God."* (St. Ignatius of Loyola).
The Good Intention should especially be made in the morning.

Eating, Drinking, Studying, Working, Playing, Resting can become Good Works, if we perform them in the state of Sanctifying Grace and with the Good Intention.
*"Whether you eat or drink, or whatsoever else you do, do all to the glory of God."* (*1 Cor.* 10:31).

## THE SACRAMENTS

A Sacrament is an outward sign instituted by Jesus Christ to give Grace.

The Sacraments have power to give Grace from the merits of Jesus Christ.

Jesus Christ gave outward signs to His Sacraments that both the Sacrament, and the Graces which it confers, may be easily recognized.

The outward sign of the Sacrament of Baptism is the pouring of the water and the speaking of the words at the same time: *I baptize thee,* etc.

The Grace which is conferred by the Sacrament of Baptism is the cleansing and sanctifying of the soul.

Sanctifying Grace is the principal Grace conferred by the Sacraments.

Some of the Sacraments give this Grace to the soul, and others increase it.

Besides Sanctifying Grace, each Sacrament confers a special Grace called Sacramental Grace.

The Sacramental Grace of the Sacrament of Penance, for example, is strength to avoid sin in the future.

Jesus Christ instituted seven Sacraments: Baptism, Confirmation, Holy Eucharist, Penance, Extreme Unction, Holy Orders, and Matrimony.

*Baptism and Penance are called* THE SACRAMENTS OF THE DEAD:
Because they take away original and mortal sin, which are the death of the soul; and
Because they give Sanctifying Grace, which is its life.

Confirmation, Holy Eucharist, Extreme Unction, Holy Orders, and Matrimony are called THE SACRAMENTS OF THE LIVING, because they must be received in the state of Sanctifying Grace.

## THE SEVEN SACRAMENTS

1. Baptism.
4. Penance.
6. Holy Orders.

*The Church is the dispenser of the fountains of the Sacraments.*
3. Holy Eucharist.

2. Confirmation.
5. Extreme Unction.
7. Matrimony.

Baptism, Confirmation, and Holy Orders imprint an indelible mark on the soul, and can only be received once.

The power of the Sacraments does not depend upon the worthiness of those who administer them, but upon the merits of Jesus Christ.

To obtain the Graces of the Sacraments, we must receive them worthily.

## THE SACRAMENT OF BAPTISM

The Sacrament of Baptism cleanses the soul from Original Sin, makes us Christians, children of God, and heirs of Heaven.

*"For as many of you as have been baptized in Christ, have put on Christ." (Gal.* 3:27).

The Sacrament of Baptism not only cleanses the soul from Original Sin, but also from all sins committed before Baptism.

It also takes away the temporal and eternal punishments due to sin.

*"Do penance, and be baptized every one of you in the name of Jesus Christ, for the remission of your sins." (Acts* 2:38).

*Baptism is most necessary for salvation:*
Because without it we cannot enter Heaven; and
Because before it, no other Sacrament can be validly
received.

*"Amen, amen I say to thee, unless a man be born again of water and the Holy Ghost, he cannot enter into the kingdom of God." (John* 3:5).

Jesus Christ instituted the Sacrament of Baptism when He declared to His Apostles:

*"Going therefore, teach ye all nations; baptizing them in the name of the Father, and of the Son, and of the Holy Ghost." (Matt.* 28:19).

*There are three kinds of Baptism:*
Baptism of water;
Baptism of desire; and
Baptism of blood.

**THE BAPTISM OF JESUS CHRIST BY JOHN THE BAPTIST** (*Mark* 1:8, 9).

Baptism of water is administered by pouring water on the head of the person to be baptized, and at the same time pronouncing the words:

*I baptize thee in the name of the Father, and of the Son, and of the Holy Ghost.*

*Baptism of desire* is an ardent wish to be baptized, and a willingness to do all that God has commanded for salvation.

*Baptism of blood* is shedding one's blood for the Faith of Jesus Christ.

Both *Baptism of desire* and *blood* are capable of producing the effects of *Baptism of water,* when it cannot be received.

The priest is the ordinary minister of the Sacrament of Baptism.

In case of necessity, ordinary natural water may be used, and anyone who has the use of reason may baptize.

*The law of the Church requires that sponsors or godparents must be practical Catholics:*
> Because they take the place of the child and answer for it; and
> Because it is their sacred duty to take care that the child is brought up in the Catholic Faith if the parents neglect this or die.

*In Baptism we promise:*
To believe firmly the teachings of the Catholic Church;
To avoid evil; and
To lead a truly Christian life.

*The name of a Saint is given at Baptism:*
That we may have a special protector in Heaven; and
That we may have a special example to follow.

Baptism can be received only once, because it imprints an indelible mark on the soul.

## THE SACRAMENT OF CONFIRMATION

Confirmation is the Sacrament by which we receive the Holy Ghost in a fuller measure than in Baptism, and are made soldiers of Jesus Christ.

*"Then they laid their hands upon them, and they received the Holy Ghost." (Acts* 8:17).

*The Sacrament of Confirmation not only brings the Holy Ghost into our soul:*

It also increases Sanctifying Grace in us;

It strengthens our Faith and gives us the strength to profess our Faith; and

It bestows upon us the gifts of the Holy Ghost.

The seven gifts of the Holy Ghost are: Wisdom, Understanding, Counsel, Fortitude, Knowledge, Piety, and Fear of the Lord. (*Is.* 11:2, 3).

To receive the Sacrament of Confirmation worthily, it is necessary to be in the state of Sanctifying Grace.

Like Baptism and Holy Orders, Confirmation imprints an indelible mark on the soul, and can be received only once.

The power to confirm belongs to the Bishops of the Catholic Church, as lawful successors of the Apostles. (*Acts* 8:17; 19:6).

When the Bishop administers Confirmation: he extends his hands over those who are to be confirmed; prays that they may receive the Holy Ghost; and then anoints their foreheads in the form of a cross, saying: *I sign thee with the Sign of the Cross, and I confirm thee with the chrism of salvation, in the name of the Father, and of the Son, and of the Holy Ghost.*

The Bishop anoints the forehead in the form of a cross to teach us that a Christian must never be ashamed of the Cross, and that he must fearlessly profess his Faith.

The Bishop gives a slight blow on the cheek when he confirms, to remind us that as soldiers of Jesus Christ, we must be ready to suffer anything, even death itself.

*"He that shall lose his life for Me, shall find it."* (*Matt.* 10:39).

*The law of the Church requires:*
That the sponsors for Confirmation be practical Catholics; and
That they have been confirmed.

*We should prepare for the reception of the Sacrament of Confirmation:*
By praying fervently to the Holy Ghost;
By making a good Confession; and
By receiving Holy Communion.

## THE SACRAMENT OF THE HOLY EUCHARIST

The Holy Eucharist is the Sacrament of the Body and Blood, Soul and Divinity of Jesus Christ under the appearances of bread and wine.

When we receive the Holy Eucharist, it is called *Holy Communion.*

When it is carried to the dying, it is called *Viaticum.*

When it is reserved in the tabernacle, it is called the *Blessed Sacrament.*

Jesus Christ promised the Holy Eucharist after the first miraculous multiplication of the loaves and fishes.

*"I am the living bread which came down from Heaven.*

*"If any man eat of this bread, he shall live forever; and the bread that I will give is My Flesh, for the life of the world." (John* 6:51, 52).

Jesus Christ instituted the Holy Eucharist at the *Last Supper* in the presence of His twelve Apostles.

*"Whilst they were at supper, Jesus took bread, blessed and broke: and gave to His disciples, and said: take ye, and eat.* THIS IS MY BODY.

*"And taking the Chalice, He gave thanks, and gave to them, saying: Drink ye all of this.*
"FOR THIS IS MY BLOOD *of the New Testament, which shall be shed for many unto remission of sins."* (*Matt.* 26:26-28) (*Mark* 14:22-24) (*1 Cor.* 11:23-26).
*"Do this for a commemoration of Me."* (*Luke* 22:19) (*1 Cor.* 11:24, 25).

When Jesus Christ pronounced the words, *This is My Body*, the bread before Him was changed into His true Body. When He pronounced the words, *This is My Blood*, the wine before Him was changed into His true Blood.

Jesus Christ instituted the Holy Eucharist by His own Almighty power.
*"All power is given to Me in Heaven and in earth."* (*Matt.* 28:18).

After Jesus Christ had changed the substance of bread and wine into the substance of His Body and Blood, there remained only the *appearances of bread and wine.*
The changing of bread and wine into the Body and Blood of Jesus Christ is called TRANSUBSTANTIATION, which means, *a change of substance.*

*The appearances of bread and wine* are everything that our senses can perceive of bread and wine, that is, *form, color, figure, taste.*
Jesus Christ remains present in the Holy Eucharist as long as the appearances of bread and wine exist.

Jesus Christ is present whole and entire under the appearance of bread and under the appearance of wine, because His Body and Blood cannot be separated.
He is, therefore, completely present in each particle of the Host and in each Drop in the Chalice.

## THE BLESSED SACRAMENT

*"Now to the king of ages, immortal, invisible, the only God, be honor and glory for ever and ever. Amen." (1 Tim. 1:17).*

Priest and Layman, King and Queen, Rich and Poor, Young and Old, White and Black pay due honor, praise and adoration to Jesus in the Blessed Sacrament.

Jesus Christ gave His Apostles the power to change bread and wine into His Body and Blood when He said to them:

*"Do this for a commemoration of Me."* (*Luke* 22:19).

The bishops and priests of the Catholic Church exercise this power, as lawful successors of the Apostles, in the Holy Sacrifice of the Mass.

*Jesus Christ instituted the Holy Eucharist:*
To abide with us on earth;
To offer Himself daily in the Sacrifice of the Mass;
To be the food of our souls in Holy Communion;
To be the pledge of eternal life; and
To fit our bodies for a glorious resurrection.

*"He that eateth My Flesh, and drinketh My Blood, hath everlasting life; and I will raise him up in the last day."* (*John* 6:55).

### HOLY COMMUNION

Holy Communion is the receiving of the Body and Blood of Jesus Christ.

To receive Holy Communion worthily, we must be in the state of Sanctifying Grace.

*He who dares to receive Holy Communion in the state of mortal sin:*
Receives the Body and Blood of Jesus Christ,
But does not receive Sanctifying Grace; and
Commits a sacrilege.

*"Whosoever shall eat this bread, or drink the chalice of the Lord unworthily, shall be guilty of the Body and of the Blood of the Lord."* (*1 Cor.* 11:27).

The Church administers Holy Communion under the form of bread alone because Jesus Christ with Body and Blood is truly present both under the appearance of bread and under the appearance of wine.

## HOLY COMMUNION

Holy Communion is the receiving of the Body and Blood of Jesus Christ.

*"I live, now not I; but Christ liveth in me."* *(Gal.* 2:20).

The happiest day in a Catholic's life is the First Holy Communion Day.

*The effects of Holy Communion are:*
It unites us most intimately with Jesus Christ;
It increases Sanctifying Grace in us;
It lessens our evil inclinations;
It cleanses us from venial sin;
It preserves us from mortal sin; and
It strengthens us in the practice of virtue.
*"He that eateth My Flesh, and drinketh My Blood, abideth in Me, and I in him." (John 6:57).*
*We should prepare for Holy Communion:*
By a good Confession;
By not partaking of food and drink from midnight;*
By making acts of Faith, Hope, Love, Adoration, Contrition, and Desire; and
By approaching the altar rail with the greatest reverence, that is, with folded hands and downcast eyes.
*After Holy Communion we should:*
Say prayers of thanksgiving;
Renew our acts of Faith, Hope, Love, Adoration, Contrition, and Desire; and
Pray to Jesus Christ for ourselves and others.

### HOLY VIATICUM

When Holy Communion is taken to those who are in danger of death, it is called *Viaticum.*
*Holy Viaticum* prepares the dying for their journey into eternity with the Body and Blood of Jesus Christ.
Relatives should not delay to call the priest when anyone is in danger of death.
Those who are in danger of death may receive the Blessed Sacrament at any time, day or night, and need not be fasting. (See p. 183 for Sickroom Table.)

---

*The Church shortened the Communion fast to 3 hours, then shortened it again to only one hour. (Water and medicine may be taken at any time before Communion.)—*Editor,* 1993.

### THE MIRACULOUS MULTIPLICATION
### OF THE LOAVES. (*John* 6).

This miracle proves the possibility of the mysterious multiplication of the Body and Blood of Jesus Christ in the Holy Eucharist.

### "HE THAT EATETH THIS BREAD SHALL
### LIVE FOREVER." (*John* 6:59).

The dying should enter eternity fortified with the Body and Blood of Jesus Christ.

## THE SACRAMENT OF PENANCE

Penance is the Sacrament in which the sins committed after Baptism are forgiven.

In the Sacrament of Penance sins are forgiven by the power of God given to the priest.

We know and believe that the priest has the power to forgive sins because Jesus Christ gave this power to His Apostles and their successors, who are the bishops and priests of the Catholic Church.

Jesus Christ instituted the Sacrament of Penance on the day of His Resurrection, when He said to His Apostles:
*"Receive ye the Holy Ghost.*
*"Whose sins you shall forgive, they are forgiven them; and whose sins you shall retain, they are retained." (John* 20:22, 23).

The power to forgive sins, like all the other powers which Jesus Christ conferred upon His Apostles, passed down to their successors, because He founded the Church for all men and all times.
*"As the Father hath sent Me, I also send you." (John* 20:21; *Matt.* 28:18, 20).

Jesus Christ forgave sins.
He forgave the sins of the man sick of the palsy, and the sins of Mary Magdalene. (*Matt.* 9; *Luke* 7).

*The Sacrament of Penance forgives:*
All mortal sins; and
All venial sins which we are sorry for and confess.

## THE INSTITUTION OF THE SACRAMENT OF PENANCE

*"Receive ye the Holy Ghost. Whose sins you shall forgive, they are forgiven them; and whose sins you shall retain, they are retained."* (*John* 20:22, 23).

*The Sacrament of Penance gives us:*
Sanctifying Grace, if it was lost;
An increase of Sanctifying Grace, if it was not lost; and
Sacramental Grace to avoid sin in the future.

*To receive the Sacrament of Penance worthily we must:*
Examine our Conscience.
Make an Act of Contrition [i.e., be sorry for our sins].
Have a firm Purpose of Amendment.
Confess our Sins to the Priest.
Make Satisfaction, or perform the Penance given to us.

### THE EXAMINATION OF CONSCIENCE

The Examination of Conscience is an earnest effort to call to mind the sins we committed since our last worthy Confession.

Before we begin to examine our conscience, we should pray to the Holy Ghost for *light* to know our sins, and *help* to make a good Confession.

*We should examine our Conscience:*
By finding out when we made our last Confession;
By asking ourselves whether or not we performed the penance which the priest gave us;
By going through the Commandments of God and the Church, and the seven capital sins; and
By considering how we have performed the duties of our state of life.

We should examine our Conscience every day, especially before we retire at night.

## CONTRITION

Contrition is supernatural sorrow for our sins. We must hate sin more than any other evil.

*There are two kinds of Contrition:*
Perfect Contrition; and
Imperfect Contrition, also called Attrition.

*Our Contrition is Perfect:*
When we are sorry because we have offended God,
    Who is the supreme Good and worthy of all love.
*"And going forth he [Peter] wept bitterly."* (*Matt.* 26:75).

Our Contrition is *Imperfect* when we are sorry for our sins out of fear of Hell and loss of Heaven.
An imperfect Contrition is sufficient for Confession.

*We should especially try to make an act of Perfect Contrition:*
When we go to Confession;
When we are in danger of death; and
If we have committed a mortal sin.

*We should be truly sorry for our sins:*
Because sin is the greatest evil in the world;
Because it is an act of disobedience against God, our
    Creator and Redeemer.

## THE PURPOSE OF AMENDMENT

*The Purpose of Amendment is a firm promise:*
To sin no more;
To avoid the occasions of sin;
To perform the penance; and
To repair all injuries.

## CONFESSION

Confession is telling our sins to a duly authorized priest for the purpose of obtaining forgiveness.

Our Confession must be *sincere* and *complete*.

Our Confession is SINCERE when we tell our sins honestly, neither exaggerating nor excusing them.

*Our Confession is* COMPLETE:
When we tell all our mortal sins;
When we tell the number and kind of our sins; and
When we tell any circumstances which change their nature to a different kind of sin.

Those who willfully conceal a mortal sin in Confession are not forgiven, and commit a sacrilege.

If we cannot remember the number of our sins, we should say how often we have sinned in a day, week, or month.

If without our fault, we should forget to confess a mortal sin, our Confession is worthy, and the sin is forgiven; but we must tell it in the next Confession.

A General Confession is one in which we repeat some or all of our former Confessions.

It is necessary when we have willfully concealed a mortal sin.

### SATISFACTION

*Satisfaction means:*
To perform the Penance which the priest gives us;
To make necessary restitution; and
To repair all injuries.

A Penance is given to us in Confession that we may satisfy, to some extent, for the temporal punishment due to us for our sins.

The temporal punishment due to sin must be satisfied for either in this life or in Purgatory.

## HOW TO GO TO CONFESSION

First, we kneel down, make the Sign of the Cross, and say to the priest: *I confess to Almighty God and to you, Father, that I have sinned.*

Second, we tell either that this is our first Confession, or how long ago we made our last Confession.

Third, we tell our sins to the priest.

Fourth, we listen to the admonition of the Priest and for the Penance.

Fifth, we do not leave the Confessional until the priest has spoken the words of Absolution and given us a sign to go.

## INDULGENCES

One of the chief means by which we can satisfy for the temporal punishment due to us for our sins is Indulgences.

An Indulgence is the remission, in whole or in part, of the temporal punishment due to our sins, outside of the Sacrament of Penance.

*There are two kinds of Indulgences:*
Plenary Indulgences; and
Partial Indulgences.

A *Plenary Indulgence* is the full remission of all the temporal punishment due to our sins.

A *Partial Indulgence* is the remission of a part of the temporal punishment due to our sins.

Jesus Christ conferred the power to grant Indulgences upon the Church when He said to St. Peter: *"And I will give to thee the keys of the Kingdom of Heaven. And whatsoever thou shalt bind upon earth, it shall be bound also in Heaven: and whatsoever thou shalt loose on earth, it shall be loosed also in Heaven."* (*Matt.* 16:19).

The Church grants Indulgences from the great Treasury of the infinite merits of Jesus Christ, and from the superabundant merits of the Blessed Virgin Mary and the Saints.

*To gain an Indulgence it is necessary:*
To be in the state of Sanctifying Grace;
To make the intention to gain it; and
To fulfill the conditions prescribed.

We can gain Indulgences for ourselves, and for the souls in Purgatory.

## JESUS CHRIST CONFERS UPON ST. PETER THE POWER TO GRANT INDULGENCES

*"And I will give to thee the keys of the Kingdom of Heaven. And whatsoever thou shall bind upon earth, it shall be bound also in Heaven: and whatsoever thou shalt loose on earth, it shall be loosed also in Heaven." (Matt. 16:19).*

## THE SACRAMENT OF EXTREME UNCTION

Extreme Unction is the Sacrament in which those who are very sick or dying receive the Grace of God for the good of body and soul, through the anointing and prayer of the priest.

*"Is any man sick among you? Let him bring in the priests of the Church, and let them pray over him, anointing him with oil in the name of the Lord.*
*"And the prayer of faith shall save the sick man: and the Lord shall raise him up: and if he be in sins, they shall be forgiven him." (James 5:14, 15).*

When the priest administers Extreme Unction, he anoints the five senses with consecrated oil.

Extreme Unction must be received in the state of Sanctifying Grace.

*The purpose of Extreme Unction is:*
To increase Sanctifying Grace;
To strengthen the soul against temptations, and especially for the struggle of death;
To remit venial sins and the temporal punishment due to sin;
To relieve the sufferings of the sick; and
To restore health, if it be the will of God.

The Sacrament of Extreme Unction should be received before the sick are in extreme danger of death.
It can be administered even though the sick cannot confess or receive Viaticum.
It can be received only once in the same illness.

See page 183 for Sickroom Table.

## EXTREME UNCTION

*"Is any man sick among you? Let him bring in the priests of the Church, and let them pray over him, anointing him with oil in the name of the Lord."* (James 5:14).

## THE SACRAMENT OF HOLY ORDERS

Holy Orders is the Sacrament by which bishops and priests and other ministers of the Church are ordained and receive Grace and Power to perform the duties of the Sacred Ministry.

*There are seven Holy Orders:*
Four minor Orders: Porter, Lector, Exorcist and Acolyte.
And three major Orders: Subdeacon, Deacon, and Priest.

Jesus Christ conferred the Order of the Holy Priesthood upon His Apostles at the Last Supper.

*"Take ye, and eat. This is My Body.*

*"Drink ye all of this. For this is My Blood of the New Testament."* (*Matt.* 26:26-28).

*"Do this for a commemoration of Me."* (*Luke* 22:19).

*The chief Powers of the Holy Priesthood are:*
To offer the Sacrifice of the Mass;
To administer the Sacraments; and
To teach.

*"As the Father hath sent Me, I also send you."* (*John* 20:21).

The Sacrament of Holy Orders is administered by the bishops of the Church, as successors of the Apostles.

*"And when they had ordained to them priests in every church, and had prayed with fasting, they commended them to the Lord, in Whom they believed."* (*Acts* 14:22).

Like Baptism and Confirmation, the Order of Holy Priesthood imprints an indelible mark on the soul.

*"Thou art a priest forever, according to the order of Melchisedech."* (*Heb.* 5:6).

We should honor the bishops and priests of the Church as the representatives of Jesus Christ.

*"Let a man so account of us as of the ministers of Christ, and the dispensers of the mysteries of God."* (*1 Cor.* 4:1).

## THE ORDAINING OF THE SEVEN DEACONS

*"These they set before the Apostles; and they praying, imposed hands upon them."* (Acts 6:6).

### THE HOLY ORDERS

1. Porter.    2. Lector.    3. Exorcist.    4. Acolyte.

5. Subdeacon.    6. Deacon.    7. Priest.

## THE SACRAMENT OF MATRIMONY

Matrimony is the Sacrament in which an unmarried man and woman are united in lawful Wedlock, and receive the Grace of God to fulfill the duties of the married state.

*Marriage is sacred:*
Because God instituted it in the Garden of Paradise; and
Because Jesus Christ raised it to the dignity of a Sacrament.
*"This is a great Sacrament; but I speak in Christ and in the Church." (Eph.* 5:32).

The bond of Marriage can only be dissolved by death.
*"What therefore God hath joined together, let no man put asunder." (Matt.* 19:6).

*The purpose of the Sacrament of Matrimony is:*
To sanctify the love of husband and wife;
To give them Grace to bear each other's weaknesses; and
To help them bring up their children in the fear and love of God.

The Bride and Bridegroom receive the Sacrament of Matrimony by declaring, in the presence of their parish priest and two witnesses, according to the Rite of the Church, that they take each other for husband and wife.

To receive the Sacrament of Matrimony worthily, it is necessary to be in the state of Sanctifying Grace, and to comply with the laws of the Church.
Catholics should receive Holy Matrimony at the Nuptial Mass.

**THE WEDDING OF MARY AND JOSEPH.** (*Matt.* 1:18).

## THE SACRAMENTALS

*The Sacramentals are:*
The Blessings and Exorcisms used by the Church; and
All those things that She blesses or consecrates to religious use.

*These things are called Sacramentals:*
Because they resemble the Sacraments; and
Because many of them are used in their administration.

The Sacramentals were instituted by the Church.
Jesus Christ sanctioned the use of Sacramentals by the many blessings He bestowed. (*Matt.* 26:26).

*The purpose of the Sacramentals is:*
To increase our devotion; and
To protect us against the powers of darkness.

The Church invokes a special *Blessing* upon those who assist at the Holy Sacrifice of the Mass, upon the bride and bridegroom, upon the sick and dying, and upon the remains of the dead.

The Church administers *Exorcism* by commanding the devil, in the name of Jesus Christ, to depart from possessed persons or things.

The Church *consecrates* certain religious, churches, chalices, altars, bells, cemeteries, and holy oils.
She *blesses* water, candles, crosses, palms, ashes, vestments, rosaries, scapulars, prayer-books, homes and foods.

To use the Sacramentals with profit, we must be in the state of Sanctifying Grace.

## THE BLESSING OF THROATS ON THE FEAST OF ST. BLAISE, FEBRUARY 3

*"Through the intercession of St. Blaise, Bishop and Martyr may God deliver thee from all disease of the Throat, and from every other evil.*

*"In the name of the Father, and of the Son, and of the Holy Ghost. Amen."*

## PRAYER

*Prayer is the lifting up of the mind and heart to God:*
To praise Him;
To thank Him; and
To ask Him for Grace.

*We should pray:*
To follow the example of Jesus Christ;
To obey His command; and
To save our soul.

*"And having dismissed the multitude, He went into a mountain alone to pray." (Matt.* 14:23).

*"Watch ye, and pray that ye enter not into temptation."* (*Matt.* 26:41).

*We must pray:*
With devotion;
With humility;
With confidence;
With resignation; and
With perseverance.

*"Amen, Amen I say to you: if you ask the Father anything in My name, He will give it to you." (John* 16:23).

*We should especially pray:*
Every morning and evening;
Before and after meals;
On Sundays and Holydays; and
In times of necessity, sickness, and temptation.

*When we do not receive what we pray for, it is either*
Because we do not ask properly; or
Because what we ask for is not in conformity with
    God's Holy Will.

The principal Prayers for a Catholic are: the Our Father, the Hail Mary, the Apostles' Creed, the Acts of Faith, Hope, Charity and Contrition, the Angelus, Grace before, and after Meals, Prayer to the Guardian Angel, the Rosary, the Stations of the Cross, and the Litanies.

## THE OUR FATHER

The Our Father is the most excellent prayer, because Jesus Christ taught it to His Apostles and commanded them to say it. (*Matt.* 6:9-13).

*Our Father, Who art in Heaven, hallowed be Thy name: Thy Kingdom come; Thy will be done on earth as it is in Heaven. Give us this day our daily bread: and forgive us our trespasses, as we forgive those who trespass against us. And lead us not into temptation: but deliver us from evil. Amen.*

## THE HAIL MARY

*The Hail Mary is composed of words addressed to the*
*Mother of God: By the Angel Gabriel;*
          *By Elizabeth, her cousin; and*
          *By the Church. (Luke 1:28; 1:42).*

Hail Mary, full of grace; the Lord is with thee; blessed
art thou among women, and blessed is the fruit of thy
womb, Jesus. Holy Mary, Mother of God, pray for us sinners, now and at the hour of our death. Amen.

## THE APOSTLES' CREED

*The Apostles' Creed is a summary of the principal doc-*
*trines of the Catholic Church. It is believed to have been*
*composed by the Apostles. (2 Tim. 1:13).*

I believe in God, the Father Almighty, Creator of
Heaven and earth: and in Jesus Christ, His only Son, our
Lord: Who was conceived by the Holy Ghost, born of the
Virgin Mary, suffered under Pontius Pilate, was crucified,
died, and was buried. He descended into hell; the third day
He arose again from the dead; He ascended into Heaven;
sitteth at the right hand of God, the Father Almighty; from
thence He shall come to judge the living and the dead.
I believe in the Holy Ghost, the holy Catholic Church, the
communion of saints, the forgiveness of sins, the resurrection of the body, and life everlasting. Amen.

## AN ACT OF FAITH

O my God! I firmly believe that Thou art one God in
three divine Persons, the Father, the Son, and the Holy
Ghost; I believe that Thy divine Son became man, and died
for our sins, and that He will come to judge the living and
the dead. I believe these and all the truths which the holy
Catholic Church teaches, because Thou hast revealed
them, Who canst neither deceive nor be deceived.

## AN ACT OF HOPE

O my God! Relying on Thine Almighty power and infinite goodness and promises, I hope to obtain pardon of my sins, the help of Thy grace and life everlasting, through the merits of Jesus Christ, my Lord and Redeemer.

## AN ACT OF LOVE

O my God! I love Thee above all things, with my whole heart and soul, because Thou art all good and worthy of all love. I love my neighbor as myself for the love of Thee. I forgive all who have injured me and ask pardon of all whom I have injured.

## AN ACT OF CONTRITION

O my God! I am heartily sorry for having offended Thee, and I detest all my sins, because I dread the loss of Heaven and the pains of Hell, but most of all because they offend Thee, my God, Who art all good, and deserving of all my love. I firmly resolve, with the help of Thy grace, to confess my sins, to do penance, and to amend my life. Amen.

## THE ANGELUS

V. The Angel of the Lord declared unto Mary.
R. And she conceived of the Holy Ghost.
   *Hail Mary, etc.*
V. Behold the handmaid of the Lord.
R. Be it done unto me according to thy word.
   *Hail Mary, etc.*
V. And the Word was made flesh. (*Genuflect.*)
R. And dwelt among us. (*Arise.*)
   *Hail Mary, etc.*
V. Pray for us, O Holy Mother of God,
R. That we may be made worthy of the promises of Christ.

### Let Us Pray

Pour forth, we beseech Thee, O Lord, Thy grace into our hearts; that we to whom the Incarnation of Christ Thy

Son was made known by the message of an angel, may by His Passion and Cross be brought to the glory of His Resurrection. Through the same Christ our Lord. Amen.

## GRACE BEFORE AND AFTER MEALS

### Before Meals

Bless us, O Lord, and these Thy gifts, which we are about to receive from Thy bounty. Through Christ Our Lord. Amen.

### After Meals

We give Thee thanks, O Almighty God, for these and all Thy gifts, which we have received from Thy bounty, through Christ Our Lord. Amen.

## PRAYER TO OUR GUARDIAN ANGEL

Angel of God, my Guardian dear,
To whom His love commits me here,
Ever this day be at my side,
To light and guard, to rule and guide. Amen.

## THE ROSARY

The Rosary is a certain form of prayer wherein we say five decades of ten *Hail Marys* with an *Our Father* beginning each ten and a *Glory be to the Father* ending each ten, while at each decade, we recall or meditate on one of the mysteries of the Redemption.

*Form of the Rosary:*
The Sign of the Cross.
The Apostles' Creed.
The Our Father and three Hail Marys.
The Glory be to the Father.
The Our Father, ten Hail Marys, and Glory be to the Father (five times).

## The Joyful Mysteries

The Annunciation.
The Visitation.
The Birth of Jesus Christ in Bethlehem.
The Presentation of the Child Jesus in the Temple.
The Finding of the Child Jesus in the Temple.

## The Sorrowful Mysteries

The Agony in the Garden of Olives.
The Scourging at the Pillar.
The Crowning with Thorns.
The Way of the Cross.
The Crucifixion on Mount Calvary.

## The Glorious Mysteries

The Resurrection.
The Ascension.
The Descent of the Holy Ghost.
The Assumption of the Blessed Virgin Mary into Heaven.
The Coronation of the Blessed Virgin Mary in Heaven.

The Mystery is announced immediately before the *Our Father* at the beginning of each decade.

### THE STATIONS OF THE CROSS

The Stations of the Cross are a meditation and prayer on fourteen prominent events in our Blessed Lord's Passion and Death.

These events are generally represented in our churches by pictures or groups of statuary figures.

## LITANIES

A Litany is a prayer composed of short invocations of God or the Saints.

*The approved Litanies of the Church are:*
The Litany of the Most Holy Name of Jesus;
The Litany of the Sacred Heart of Jesus;
The Litany of the Blessed Virgin Mary;
The Litany of St. Joseph; and
The Litany of the Saints.

## CATHOLIC DEVOTIONS

*There are four prominent Catholic Devotions:*
The Sacred Heart Devotion held in June, and on the First Friday of the month;

The May Devotion, dedicated to the Blessed Virgin Mary;

The Rosary Devotion, also dedicated to the Blessed Virgin Mary, and especially held during the month of October; and

The Devotion to St. Joseph, held in March.

# APPENDIX: LIST OF THE POPES

1. St. Peter, d. 67
2. St. Linus, 67-79
3. St. Anacletus I, 79-90
4. St. Clement I, 90-99
5. St. Evaristus, 99-107
6. St. Alexander I, 107-16
7. St. Sixtus I, 116-25
8. St. Telesphorus, 125-36
9. St. Hyginus, 136-40
10. St. Pius, 140-54
11. St. Anicetus, 154-65
12. St. Soter, 165-74
13. St. Eleutherius, 174-89
14. St. Victor, 189-98
15. St. Zephyrinus, 198-217
16. St. Callistus I, 217-22
17. St. Urban I, 222-30
18. St. Pontian, 230-35
19. St. Antherus, 235-36
20. St. Fabian, 236-50
21. St. Cornelius, 251-53
22. St. Lucius I, 253-54
23. St. Stephen I, 254-57
24. St. Sixtus II, 257-58
25. St. Dionysius, 259-68
26. St. Felix I, 269-74
27. St. Eutychian, 275-83
28. St. Caius, 283-96
29. St. Marcellinus, 296-304
30. St. Marcellus I, 304-09
31. St. Eusebius, 309-11
32. St. Melchiades, 311-13
33. St. Sylvester I, 314-35
34. St. Marcus, 336
35. St. Julius I, 337-52
36. St. Liberius, 352-66
37. St. Damasus I, 366-84
38. St. Siricius, 384-98
39. St. Anastasius I, 398-401
40. St. Innocent I, 402-17
41. St. Zosimus, 417-18
42. St. Boniface I, 418-22
43. St. Celestine I, 422-32
44. St. Sixtus III, 432-40
45. St. Leo I, 440-61
46. St. Hilarius, 461-68
47. St. Simplicius, 468-83

48. St. Felix II, 483-92
49. St. Gelasius I, 492-96
50. St. Anastasius II, 496-98
51. Symmachus, 498-514
52. St. Hormisdas, 514-23
53. St. John I, 523-26
54. St. Felix III, 526-30
55. Boniface II, 530-32
56. John II, 533-35
57. St. Agapetus I, 535-36
58. St. Silverius, 536-38
59. Vigilius, 538-555
60. Pelagius I, 556-61
61. John III, 561-74
62. Benedict I, 575-79
63. Pelagius II, 579-90
64. St. Gregory I, 590-604
65. Sabinianus, 604-06
66. Boniface III, 607
67. St. Boniface IV, 608-15
68. St. Deusdedit, 615-18
69. Boniface V, 619-25
70. Honorius I, 625-38
71. Severinus, 638-40
72. John IV, 640-42
73. Theodore I, 642-49
74. St. Martin I, 649-55
75. St. Eugene I, 655-57
76. St. Vitalian, 657-72
77. Adeodatus, 672-76
78. Donus, 676-78
79. St. Agatho, 678-81
80. St. Leo II, 682-83
81. St. Benedict II, 684-85
82. John V, 685-86
83. Conon, 686-87
84. St. Sergius I, 687-701
85. John VI, 701-05
86. John VII, 705-07
87. Sisinnius, 708
88. Constantine, 708-15
89. St. Gregory II, 715-31
90. St. Gregory III, 731-41
91. St. Zacharias, 741-52
92. St. Stephen II, 752-57
93. St. Paul I, 757-67
94. Stephen III, 768-72

95. Adrian I, 772-95
96. St. Leo III, 795-816
97. St. Stephen IV, 816-17
98. St. Paschal I, 817-24
99. Eugene II, 824-27
100. Valentine, 827
101. Gregory IV, 827-44
102. Sergius II, 844-47
103. St. Leo IV, 847-55
104. Benedict III, 855-58
105. St. Nicholas I, 858-67
106. Adrian II, 867-72
107. John VIII, 872-82
108. Marinus I, 882-84
109. Adrian III, 884-85
110. Stephen V, 885-91
111. Formosus, 891-96
112. Boniface VI, 896
113. Stephen VI, 896-97
114. Romanus, 897
115. Theodore II, 897
116. John IX, 898-900
117. Benedict IV, 900-03
118. Leo V, 903
119. Christopher, 903-04
120. Sergius III, 904-11
121. Anastasius III, 911-13
122. Lando, 913-14
123. John X, 914-28
124. Leo VI, 928
125. Stephen VII, 928-31
126. John XI, 931-36
127. Leo VII, 936-39
128. Stephen VIII, 939-42
129. Marinus II, 942-46
130. Agapetus II, 946-55
131. John XII, 955-64
132. Leo VIII, 964-65
133. Benedict V, 965
134. John XIII, 965-72
135. Benedict VI, 973-74
136. Benedict VII, 974-83
137. John XIV, 983-84
138. Boniface VII, 984-85
139. John XV, 985-96
140. Gregory V, 996-99
141. Sylvester II, 999-1003
142. John XVII, 1003
143. John XVIII, 1003-09

144. Sergius IV, 1009-12
145. Benedict VIII, 1012-24
146. John XIX, 1024-32
147. Benedict IX, 1032-45
148. Gregory VI, 1045-46
149. Clement II, 1046-47
150. Damasus II, 1048
151. St. Leo IX, 1049-54
152. Victor II, 1055-57
153. Stephen IX, 1057-58
154. Benedict X, 1058-59
155. Nicholas II, 1059-61
156. Alexander II, 1061-73
157. St. Gregory VII,
     1073-85
158. Victor III, 1087
159. Urban II, 1088-99
160. Pascal II, 1099-1118
161. Gelasius II, 1118-19
162. Callistus II, 1119-24
163. Honorius II, 1124-30
164. Innocent II, 1130-43
165. Celestine II, 1143-44
166. Lucius, 1144-45
167. Eugene III, 1145-1153
168. Anastasius IV, 1153-54
169. Adrian IV, 1154-59
170. Alexander III, 1159-81
171. Lucius III, 1181-85
172. Urban III, 1185-87
173. Gregory VIII, 1187
174. Clement III, 1187-91
175. Celestine III, 1191-98
176. Innocent III, 1198-1216
177. Honorius III, 1216-27
178. Gregory IX, 1227-41
179. Celestine IV, 1241
180. Innocent IV, 1243-54
181. Alexander IV, 1254-61
182. Urban IV, 1261-64
183. Clement IV, 1265-68
184. St. Gregory X, 1271-76
185. Innocent V, 1276
186. Adrian V, 1276
187. John XXI, 1276-77
188. Nicholas III, 1277-80
189. Martin IV, 1281-85
190. Honorius IV, 1285-87
191. Nicholas IV, 1288-92

192. St. Celestine V, 1294
193. Boniface VIII, 1294-1303
194. Benedict XI, 1303-04
195. Clement V, 1305-14
196. John XXII, 1316-34
197. Benedict XII, 1334-42
198. Clement VI, 1342-52
199. Innocent VI, 1352-62
200. Urban V, 1362-70
201. Gregory XI, 1370-78
202. Urban VI, 1378-89
203. Boniface IX, 1389-1404
204. Innocent VII, 1404-06
205. Gregory XII, 1406-09
206. Alexander V, 1409-10
207. John XXIII, 1410-15
208. Martin V, 1417-31
209. Eugene IV, 1431-47
210. Nicholas V, 1447-55
211. Callistus III, 1455-58
212. Pius II, 1458-64
213. Paul II, 1464-71
214. Sixtus IV, 1471-84
215. Innocent VIII, 1484-92
216. Alexander VI, 1492-1503
217. Pius III, 1503
218. Julius II, 1503-13
219. Leo X, 1513-21
220. Adrian VI, 1522-23
221. Clement VII, 1523-34
222. Paul III, 1534-49
223. Julius III, 1550-55
224. Marcellus II, 1555
225. Paul IV, 1555-59
226. Pius IV, 1559-65
227. St. Pius V, 1566-72

228. Gregory XIII, 1572-85
229. Sixtus V, 1585-90
230. Urban VII, 1590
231. Gregory XIV, 1590-91
232. Innocent IX, 1591
233. Clement VIII, 1592-1605
234. Leo XI, 1605
235. Paul V, 1605-21
236. Gregory XV, 1621-23
237. Urban VIII, 1623-44
238. Innocent X, 1644-55
239. Alexander VII, 1655-67
240. Clement IX, 1667-69
241. Clement X, 1670-76
242. Innocent XI, 1676-89
243. Alexander VIII, 1689-91
244. Innocent XII, 1691-1700
245. Clement XI, 1700-21
246. Innocent XIII, 1721-24
247. Benedict XIII, 1724-30
248. Clement XII, 1730-40
249. Benedict XIV, 1740-58
250. Clement XIII, 1758-69
251. Clement XIV, 1769-74
252. Pius VI, 1775-99
253. Pius VII, 1800-23
254. Leo XII, 1823-29
255. Pius VIII, 1829-30
256. Gregory XVI, 1831-46
257. Pius IX, 1846-78
258. Leo XIII, 1878-1903
259. Pius X, 1903-14
260. Benedict XV, 1914-22
261. Pius XI, 1922-1939
262. Pius XII, 1939*

NOTE: The list of the Popes is given to trace the lineage of the successors in the Papacy from St. Peter, the first visible Head of the Church.

*"And I say to thee: That thou art Peter: and upon this rock I will build My Church, and the Gates of Hell shall not prevail against it." (Matt. 16:18).*

*"And behold I am with you all days, even to the consummation of the world." (Matt. 28:20).*

*Editor's Addition (1993): 262. Pius XII, 1939-1958; 263. John XXIII, 1958-1963; 264. Paul VI, 1963-1978; 265. John Paul I, 1978; 266. John Paul II, 1978-

## LIST OF THE CHIEF CHRISTIAN RELIGIONS*
## AND THEIR FOUNDERS

| Religion | Founder | Year | Place of Origin |
|---|---|---|---|
| Catholic Church | Jesus Christ | 33 | Palestine |

| Christian Sects | Founder | Year | Place of Origin |
|---|---|---|---|
| Anabaptists | Nicholas Stork | 1521 | Germany |
| Lutherans | Martin Luther | 1524 | Germany |
| Episcopalians | Henry VIII | 1534 | England |
| United Congregationalists | Celerius | 1540 | Germany |
| Presbyterians | General Assembly | 1560 | Scotland |
| Congregationalists | Robert Browne | 1583 | England |
| Baptists | Roger Williams | 1639 | Rhode Island |
| Quakers | George Fox | 1647 | England |
| Quakers | William Penn | 1681 | America |
| Methodist Episcopal | John Wesley | 1739 | England |
| Free Will Baptists | Benjamin Randall | 1780 | New Hampshire |
| Campbellites | Alexander Campbell | 1813 | Virginia |
| Seventh-Day Baptists | General Conference | 1833 | America |
| Christian Science | Mary Baker Eddy | 1879 | Boston |
| Christian Catholic Church | John Alexander Dowie | 1890 | Zion City |

---

*Since this book was written there have arisen many, many more sects.—*Editor,* 1993.

## HOW TO PREPARE A SICKROOM TABLE

| | | |
|---|---|---|
| 2. Candle | 1. Crucifix | 2. Candle |
| 3. Salt | 5. Glass of Water | 7. Holy Water |
| | 4. Spoon | 6. Napkin |
| 8. Plate with Lemon and Bread | | 9. Plate with Cotton |

NOTE: This is the proper preparation for *Extreme Unction* and *Viaticum*. For *Holy Communion* or *Viaticum*, COTTON, SALT, BREAD, AND LEMON are not needed.

When the priest carries the Blessed Sacrament to a home, it is fitting to meet him at the door with a *lighted candle*.

# INDEX

*If you have enjoyed this book, consider making your next selection from among the following . . .*

St. Philomena—The Wonder-Worker. *O'Sullivan* . . . . . . . . . . . . . . . . . . 6.00
The Facts About Luther. *Msgr. Patrick O'Hare* . . . . . . . . . . . . . . . . . . 13.50
Little Catechism of the Curé of Ars. *St. John Vianney* . . . . . . . . . . . . . 5.50
The Curé of Ars—Patron Saint of Parish Priests. *Fr. B. O'Brien* . . . . . . 4.50
Saint Teresa of Ávila. *William Thomas Walsh* . . . . . . . . . . . . . . . . . . 18.00
Isabella of Spain: The Last Crusader. *William Thomas Walsh* . . . . . . . . 20.00
Characters of the Inquisition. *William Thomas Walsh* . . . . . . . . . . . . . . 12.50
Blood-Drenched Altars—Cath. Comment. on Hist. Mexico. *Kelley* . . . . 18.00
The Four Last Things—Death, Judgment, Hell, Heaven. *Fr. von Cochem* 5.00
Confession of a Roman Catholic. *Paul Whitcomb* . . . . . . . . . . . . . . . . . 1.25
The Catholic Church Has the Answer. *Paul Whitcomb* . . . . . . . . . . . . . 1.25
The Sinner's Guide. *Ven. Louis of Granada* . . . . . . . . . . . . . . . . . . . . . 12.00
True Devotion to Mary. *St. Louis De Montfort* . . . . . . . . . . . . . . . . . . 7.00
Life of St. Anthony Mary Claret. *Fanchón Royer* . . . . . . . . . . . . . . . . 12.50
Autobiography of St. Anthony Mary Claret . . . . . . . . . . . . . . . . . . . . . 12.00
I Wait for You. *Sr. Josefa Menendez* . . . . . . . . . . . . . . . . . . . . . . . . . . .75
Words of Love. *Menendez, Betrone, Mary of the Trinity* . . . . . . . . . . . . 5.00
Little Lives of the Great Saints. *John O'Kane Murray* . . . . . . . . . . . . . 16.50
Prayer—The Key to Salvation. *Fr. Michael Müller* . . . . . . . . . . . . . . . . 7.00
Sermons on Prayer. *St. Francis de Sales* . . . . . . . . . . . . . . . . . . . . . . . 3.50
Sermons on Our Lady. *St. Francis de Sales* . . . . . . . . . . . . . . . . . . . . . 9.00
Passion of Jesus and Its Hidden Meaning. *Fr. Groenings, S.J.* . . . . . . . . 12.50
The Victories of the Martyrs. *St. Alphonsus Liguori* . . . . . . . . . . . . . . . 8.50
Canons and Decrees of the Council of Trent. *Transl. Schroeder* . . . . . . 12.50
Sermons of St. Alphonsus Liguori for Every Sunday . . . . . . . . . . . . . . . 16.50
A Catechism of Modernism. *Fr. J. B. Lemius* . . . . . . . . . . . . . . . . . . . 4.00
Alexandrina—The Agony and the Glory. *Johnston* . . . . . . . . . . . . . . . . 4.00
Blessed Margaret of Castello. *Fr. William Bonniwell* . . . . . . . . . . . . . . 6.00
The Ways of Mental Prayer. *Dom Vitalis Lehodey* . . . . . . . . . . . . . . . . 11.00
Fr. Paul of Moll. *van Speybrouck* . . . . . . . . . . . . . . . . . . . . . . . . . . . 9.00
St. Francis of Paola. *Simi and Segreti* . . . . . . . . . . . . . . . . . . . . . . . . 7.00
Communion Under Both Kinds. *Michael Davies* . . . . . . . . . . . . . . . . . 1.50
Abortion: Yes or No? *Dr. John L. Grady, M.D.* . . . . . . . . . . . . . . . . . . 1.50
The Story of the Church. *Johnson, Hannan, Dominica* . . . . . . . . . . . . . 16.50
Religious Liberty. *Michael Davies* . . . . . . . . . . . . . . . . . . . . . . . . . . . 1.50
Hell Quizzes. *Radio Replies Press* . . . . . . . . . . . . . . . . . . . . . . . . . . . 1.00
Indulgence Quizzes. *Radio Replies Press* . . . . . . . . . . . . . . . . . . . . . . 1.00
Purgatory Quizzes. *Radio Replies Press* . . . . . . . . . . . . . . . . . . . . . . . 1.00
Virgin and Statue Worship Quizzes. *Radio Replies Press* . . . . . . . . . . . 1.00
The Holy Eucharist. *St. Alphonsus* . . . . . . . . . . . . . . . . . . . . . . . . . . . 8.50
Meditation Prayer on Mary Immaculate. *Padre Pio* . . . . . . . . . . . . . . . 1.25
Little Book of the Work of Infinite Love. *de la Touche* . . . . . . . . . . . . . 2.00
Textual Concordance of The Holy Scriptures. *Williams* . . . . . . . . . . . . 35.00
Douay-Rheims Bible. *Leatherbound* . . . . . . . . . . . . . . . . . . . . . . . . . . 35.00
The Way of Divine Love. *Sister Josefa Menendez* . . . . . . . . . . . . . . . . 17.50
The Way of Divine Love. (pocket, unabr.). *Menendez* . . . . . . . . . . . . . 8.50
Mystical City of God—Abridged. *Ven. Mary of Agreda* . . . . . . . . . . . 18.50

Prices guaranteed through December 31, 1995.

**At your Bookdealer or direct from the Publisher.**

Prices guaranteed through December 31, 1995.